MW00772736

Praise for *The Characters of Creation*

What we believe about origins necessarily influences everything else we believe. The Bible gives us the true story of how we all got here, and in *The Characters of Creation* Dan Darling does a great job of explaining that story and reminding us why it matters. Like his previous books in this series, Dan focuses on the characters—the people—who were key participants in the story of creation. In so doing, he helps us to better focus attention on the Main Character: the One who created all things and who will one day finish His work of re-creation, to the eternal praise of His glory.

NATHAN A. FINN

Provost and Dean of the University Faculty, North Greenville University

There are big questions that everyone has to answer: Where am I from? Where am I going? What's wrong with the world? What's the solution? All of these big questions are answered in the early chapters of Genesis. That is why I am really excited about *The Characters of Creation* and Dan Darling's fresh perspective on the origin story. Read this book and learn how the stories of the earliest people to inhabit the world connect with the story of your life.

JONATHAN AKIN

Vice President for Church Relations and Campus Ministries at Carson-Newman University

As always, Daniel Darling masterfully unpacks the beauty inherent in Scripture and helps readers dig deeper into important people, places, and narratives—stories that can sometimes become clouded, overlooked, and misunderstood. In *The Characters of Creation*, he helps us better comprehend Adam, Eve, Noah, and the beginnings of human history. This is a must-read book for anyone who seeks to explore and better connect with the people at the forefront of human history—and with the Lord.

BILLY HALLOWELL
Digital host/journalist, CBN News

Reading a Dan Darling book is like having a long conversation with a friend. A very bright, serious-minded, and sometimes quirky friend. I love Dan's special insights into God's Word and the gospel. This book takes you back to the beginning of everything and sheds new light on the people—some you've heard of, others you haven't—and all that happened to them back there. Get ready for a unique, enlightening, and really sweet experience.

ROBERT WOLGEMUTH
Bestselling author

THE
CHARACTERS
of CREATION

The Men, Women, Creatures, and Serpent
Present at the Beginning of the World

DANIEL DARLING

MOODY PUBLISHERS

CHICAGO

Unless otherwise noted, all Scripture quotations are taken from the Christian Standard Bible®, copyright ©2017 by Holman Bible Publishers. Used by permission. Christian Standard Bible® and CSB® are federally registered trademarks of Holman Bible Publishers.

Scripture quotations marked (NIV) are taken from the Holy Bible, New International Version®, NIV®. Copyright © 1973, 1978, 1984, 2011 by Biblica, Inc.™ Used by permission of Zondervan. All rights reserved worldwide. www.zondervan.com The "NIV" and "New International Version" are trademarks registered in the United States Patent and Trademark Office by Biblica, Inc.™

Scripture quotations marked (ESV) are from the *ESV® Bible (The Holy Bible, English Standard Version®)*, Copyright © 2001 by Crossway, a publishing ministry of Good News Publishers. Used by permission. All rights reserved.

Scripture quotations marked (KJV) are taken from the King James Version.

Published in association with the literary agency of Wolgemuth & Associates.

Edited by Elizabeth Cody Newenhuyse
Interior design: Puckett Smartt
Cover design: Thinkpen Design
Cover illustration of fox silhouette copyright © 2020 by Martinus Sumbaji / Shutterstock (1195534375).
Cover illustration of tigers copyright © 2020 by evgo1977 / Shutterstock (1279375279).
Cover illustration of man and staff silhouette copyright © 2020 by ArtMari / Shutterstock (1734428030).
Cover illustration of fighting men copyright © 2020 by ArtMari / Shutterstock (2020134047).
Cover photo of couple copyright © 2020 by Dudarev Mikhail / Shutterstock (77358031).
Cover photo of Roman soldier copyright © 2020 by Book Cover Photos / Shutterstock (1061561999).
All rights reserved for the images listed above.

Library of Congress Cataloging-in-Publication Data

Names: Darling, Daniel, 1978- author.
Title: The characters of creation : the men, women, creatures, and serpent present at the beginning of the world / Daniel Darling.
Description: Chicago : Moody Publishers, 2022. | Includes bibliographical references. | Summary: "In The Characters of Creation, Daniel Darling re-introduces readers to the story they thought they knew. He explains the Bible's story of how we got here and how things got messed up, and gives fresh insights into the first people in God's unfolding plan of redemption--from Adam and Eve, The Serpent, Cain and Abel, and Noah"-- Provided by publisher.
Identifiers: LCCN 2022002436 (print) | LCCN 2022002437 (ebook) | ISBN 9780802425010 (paperback) | ISBN 9780802475398
Subjects: LCSH: Creationism. | Creation. | Bible. Genesis--Criticism, interpretation, etc. | BISAC: RELIGION / Christian Theology / History | RELIGION / Christian Living / Inspirational
Classification: LCC BS651 .D324 2022 (print) | LCC BS651 (ebook) | DDC 231.7/65--dc23/eng/20220210
LC record available at https://lccn.loc.gov/2022002436
LC ebook record available at https://lccn.loc.gov/2022002437

Originally delivered by fleets of horse-drawn wagons, the affordable paperbacks from D. L. Moody's publishing house resourced the church and served everyday people. Now, after more than 125 years of publishing and ministry, Moody Publishers' mission remains the same—even if our delivery systems have changed a bit. For more information on other books (and resources) created from a biblical perspective, go to www.moodypublishers.com or write to:

Moody Publishers
820 N. LaSalle Boulevard
Chicago, IL 60610

1 3 5 7 9 10 8 6 4 2

Printed in the United States of America

This book is dedicated to my Uncle Jim, who passed away from Alzheimer's while I was making final edits. Uncle Jim expressed his love for God's good creation with his amazing photography of sunsets and water and landscapes and his love for fishing in Northern Minnesota. Most of all, Uncle Jim lived out God's purposes for his life as a faithful husband, father, and churchman. He's with Jesus now, awaiting that promised resurrection at the end of the age. Uncle Jim, I can't wait to see you one day.

CONTENTS

In the Beginning, God

The hero of creation is God.[1]

—BRUCE WALTKE

A few days before I sat down to write this book, I bought a truck. I've been wanting one for a long time, and with my oldest daughter now driving my sedan, this was my chance. I found a pretty good deal. I have to say it feels really good. I've been driving down the road blasting "Boy Gets a Truck" by Keith Urban and feeling like I'm on top of the world.

There was one small fix I made, a cosmetic adjustment that made my wife smile and my almost-teenage son excited. The Ford logo on the front of the truck was worn, to the point where you could make out a faint image of the iconic insignia, but couldn't quite see it in all of its glory. So I did what every self-respecting Ford owner would have done. I Googled "Ford logo for F-150" and had it shipped from Amazon.

Well, yesterday it arrived, and I popped it on that front grille. And yes, the Keith Urban is cranked up a little louder. I feel good.

Something occurred to me as I was doing all this. Ask a proud Ford owner, and they will tell you why Ford trucks are the best. It's like this with any of the products we enjoy. Seeing that Apple on the back of my laptop makes me feel warm inside and confident that I'm using a quality product. And don't even get me started on off-brand peanut butter that's not Jif. I can't even!

That legendary blue Ford symbol, that iconic Apple, the Nike Swoosh—they all communicate one message: *This product was made by someone you trust.*

Imagine, for a moment, if when I first pulled up and showed all my buddies my new truck (a thing that guys do, by the way), one of them asked, "What did you buy?" and I say, "Oh, I don't know who makes it. I just like it." Or if I said something like, "We are not really all that clear about how it was actually constructed. I just know it drives really well."

My buddies would think I inhaled some truck fumes. Nobody says that. We are proud of the maker and designer of our products. I mean, I went on Amazon and bought a new logo plate for this very purpose because I want the world to know who made my truck.

I promise this isn't a book about brands and logos. The only reason I'm talking about it is simply this: If a two-ton hunk of aluminum and steel like my Ford declares its maker, how much so does a complex world point toward a designer? This is what creation is all about, really. King David wrote in Psalm 19:1 that "the heavens declare the glory of God, and the expanse proclaims the work of his hands." It's as if this world, the universe, the cosmos, and the creatures in this world are not-so-subtly shouting that we have been carefully crafted and made and designed. Creation is about declaring that *we* have not just arrived on the doorstep of destiny, the product of mysterious explosion of atoms and chemicals, but are the intentional design of a loving Creator.

✦ God Is the Story of Creation ✦

This reality is why I've always been fascinated by Genesis. Every single question I have about the world, about myself, about almost everything, is rooted in this beautiful book of beginnings. That is why I felt compelled to follow up *The Characters of Christmas* and *The Characters of Easter* with a new project on the people who were there when it all began.

But before we can understand the characters of creation, we must first bow before the Author of Creation. God is not just another actor in this drama, a figure we mold and massage into a deity of our liking. Instead, the Bible opens by describing the formation of the world as an act that begins with the One who had no beginning, who is always there. Jesus would later testify to the religious leaders that "before Abraham was, *I am.*" Theologians call this God's "pre-existence."

I've been reading Genesis 1 for four decades, and yet every time my eyes fall on those words, I can't help but be met by awe and wonder. *In the beginning . . . God.* I love what British Old Testament scholar Derek Kidner writes: "It's no accident that *God* is the subject of the first sentence of the Bible, for this word dominates the whole chapter and catches the eye at every point of the page."[2] Physicist Arthur Compton once remarked that "in the beginning God" is a phrase that is "the most tremendous ever penned."[3]

Why are these four simple words at the beginning of our Bibles "the most tremendous ever penned"? The Bible is making the claim that the entire cosmos and everything in it had a purposeful and orderly origin—and that God was there. In other words, there was no violent clash of equal deities vying for supremacy. There was no random eruption of atoms that resulted in the order and design of the universe. The Bible asserts that a loving Father formed the universe and carefully crafted the human beings who bear His image.

"I make known the end from the beginning, from ancient times, what is still to come" (Isa. 46:10 NIV); "I am the first and I am the last," God whispers to the prophet Isaiah (Isa. 44:6). John reminds us that God was "in the beginning" (John 1). The psalmist declares, "Before the mountains were born, before you gave birth to the earth and the world, from eternity to eternity, you are God" (Ps. 90:2).

From eternity to eternity, you are God. For finite creatures, this is hard to wrap our minds around. Everything in our lives had a beginning and has a fixed endpoint, but God is eternal and transcendent. He is outside of time. Theologian John Frame writes that "it is significant that the world has a beginning, and that God exists before that beginning . . . the Creator precedes the creation."[4]

We cannot possibly comprehend the fullness of who God is. Throughout the ages our most brilliant minds have merely scratched the surface. And yet as we begin a book about the characters of creation it is important for us to pause and dwell on God for a moment. We must understand that God is no mere character, but He is the story, the author, the beginning of creation. He's not one in a pantheon of feuding gods as the first readers of Moses's words in Genesis may have imagined. He's not "one with the universe" as many religions today might muse. He is not a figment of our imagination, a kind of shape-shifting deity who conforms around our preferences.

God stands *outside* of His creation; He is *other* than His creation; He is *above* His creation.

This short phrase also tells us *how* God created. *In the beginning, God created* implies that God began His creative acts with . . . nothing.

Stay with me here for a moment. In one sense, the act of creating is something shared by both creator and creation, especially humans (more on that in a future chapter). Right now, I'm creating this chapter. I'm making something new that didn't exist before. You create in your daily life, whether building furniture or launching new projects or filling out spreadsheets or baking a cake.

There is a vast difference, though, between our creation and God's. When we create, we start with raw materials. I start every book with knowledge gained by other books, with a MacBook and software, with a mind crafted by God in my mother's womb. When a carpenter crafts furniture, he starts with raw or repurposed wood. When a baker makes a cake, she begins with sugar and flour and yeast and a thousand other ingredients.

Let's go back now to my beloved Ford F-150. This truck's construction points back to its creator. Yet we all know the employees in the Ford factory began with raw materials, like aluminum, steel, leather, glass, and plastic. In fact, as I'm writing, there are thousands of brand-new cars on lots all over the world right now that can't be driven or sold because there is a microchip shortage. The Ford F-150 and every other car depends on the availability of stuff that already exists.

> God began His creative acts with . . . nothing.

God's creative acts at the beginning of the world were different. Theologians have a term for this: creation *ex nihilo*, a Latin word that simply means "out of nothing, something." In other words, God didn't start with raw materials. God didn't start with a lump of clay. God started with nothing.

The rest of the Scriptures illuminate this. "For he spoke, and it came into being; he commanded, and it came into existence," we read in Psalm 33:9; while Psalm 90:2 declares, "Before the mountains were born, before you gave birth to the earth and the world, from eternity to eternity, you are God." In response to Job's questions, God answered him by reminding him of His creative acts:

> *Who fixed its dimensions? Certainly you know!*
> *Who stretched a measuring line across it?*
> *What supports its foundations?*
> *Or who laid its cornerstone*
> *while the morning stars sang together*
> *and all the sons of God shouted for joy?*
>
> *Who enclosed the sea behind doors*
> *when it burst from the womb,*
> *when I made the clouds its garment*
> *and total darkness its blanket,*
> *when I determined its boundaries*
> *and put its bars and doors in place,*
> *when I declared, "You may come this far, but no farther;*
> *your proud waves stop here"? (Job 38:5–11)*

The New Testament also illuminates creation *ex nihilo.* John asserts that "all things were created through him, and apart from him not one thing was created that has been created" (John 1:3). Paul tells us that "everything was created by him, in heaven and on earth, the visible and the invisible, whether thrones or dominions or rulers or authorities—all things have been created through him and for him" (Col. 1:16) and that "For from him and through him and to him are all things" (Rom. 11:36). God "calls things into existence that do not

exist" (Rom. 4:17). The writer of Hebrews says, "by faith we understand that the universe was created by the word of God, so that what is
seen was made from things that are not visible" (Heb.11:3).

Kidner describes God's creation in this way: "Our commands,
even at their most precise, are mere outlines: they rely on existing
materials and agencies to embody them, and the craftsman himself
works with what he finds, to produce what he only knows in part. The
Creator, on the other hand, in willing an end willed every smallest
means to it, his thought shaping itself exactly to the least cell and atom,
and his creative word wholly meaningful."[5] Another theologian, John
Frame, writes: "Creation is an act of God alone, by which for his own
glory, he brings into existence everything in the universe, things that
had no existence prior to his creative word."[6]

Even the original Hebrew word used for God's creative acts, *bara,*
gives these acts distinction from the way humans make things. This
word is only ever used in Scripture in relation to God's creation. This
means God is, as one theologian says, the "creative and binding force
of life."[7]

If this is true, if God is the "creative and binding force of life," then
the only right response is to lean in and learn more about our Maker.
Too often our approach to Genesis, our approach to creation, bogs
down in either shrugging dismissal of or intramural debates about the
exact age of the earth or other tiresome debates. But I believe the first
objective, when the Spirit inspired Moses to pen the words of Genesis, was to make a statement that there is a God who is always there,
who breathed out creation with His words, who fashioned human
beings with care and concern, who was at the beginning with an end
in mind, who is Lord of history, Lord of creation.

Creation matters because it helps correct ideas about God, about humanity, and about the cosmos. The words of this ancient text came to an ancient Near East shaped by mystical and supernatural ideas, a framework that involved jealous and capricious deities and to the people of God who had spent centuries embedded in an Egyptian culture filled with false notions of the supernatural. Having seen God demonstrate His superiority over the gods of Egypt, Moses now intended for His people to learn the truth about who God is and who they were created to be.

David Atkinson explains how Genesis contrasts with the origin stories told in ancient Mesopotamia:

> Whereas the *Enuma Elish* talks about many gods, Genesis proclaims a majestic monotheism: there is one God. Whereas in the Babylonian stories the divine spirit and cosmic matter exist side by side from eternity, Genesis proclaims God's majestic distinction from everything else which in sovereign power he creates, and which depends on him for existence. Whereas in the Near Eastern mythology the sun, moon, stars and sea monsters are seen as powerful gods, Genesis tells us that they are merely creatures. . . . Whereas in the Mesopotamian myths, light emanates from the gods, in the Genesis narrative, God creates light by the power of his word . . . Genesis 1 sings the praise of the majestic Creator of all. It speaks of his life-giving power. It also gives a profound significance to human life . . . One can imagine what a rock of stability this chapter would have provided for the people of God when faced with the lure of pagan myths around them.[8]

We are so many centuries removed from the time when Moses, inspired by the Holy Spirit, wrote about how the world began—and yet we are no less lured by our own pagan myths. The biblical story of creation is as relevant today as it was then and is a welcome antidote to the false ideas that pervade our world, ideas that afflict people with confusion and despair. The God of creation is not the God of materialism, that endless treadmill that sees this physical world and the acquiring of riches as the only end in life. The God of creation is not the God of pantheism and Eastern religions that diminishes human uniqueness and sees God and the universe as one united whole. If you've ever heard someone say, "The universe is telling me something," you've arrived at a soft (and quite impersonal) pantheism. The God of creation is also not the God of dualism, which has God and the cosmos running on parallel tracks, nor is the God of creation the God of deism, a kind of absent deity who constructed a world over which he has no power.[9]

Genesis gives us something so unique for its time and so unique for our modern world: a God both transcendent and near, both powerful and personal. Genesis gives us a God who has chosen to speak. "God speaks. He is a talking God. The first thing he does is speak and by his powerful word calls the universe into existence,"[10] says theologian D. A. Carson. Creation is a powerful way in which God communicates. The writer of Psalm 19 says, "The heavens declare the glory of God, and the expanse proclaims the work of his hands." It's a powerful testimony, but it's far from the only way God speaks. The writer of Hebrews says that God also speaks through His written Word and in the person of Jesus Christ:

> *Long ago God spoke to our ancestors by the prophets at different times and in different ways. In these last days, he has spoken to us by his Son. God has appointed him heir of all things and made the universe through him. The Son is the radiance of God's glory and*

the exact expression of his nature, sustaining all things by his
powerful word. (Heb. 1:1–3)

The Christian story gives us an intensely personal God, the three-in-one triune Godhead, who not only created this world but intervenes in this world and sustains the world and is leading the world toward glory. The Father, Son, and Spirit were all active in creation. Genesis 1 tells us the Spirit hovered over the waters. And later passages in Scripture assert that Jesus Christ was the active agent in creation. This is the meaning of John's opening words in his gospel, when he points to Jesus of Nazareth, the God-man born of Mary, and says of Him that He was "with God in the beginning" and that "all things were created through him, and apart from him not one thing was created that has been created." This is the meaning of Paul's words, "For everything was created by him, in heaven and on earth, the visible and the invisible, whether thrones or dominions or rulers or authorities—all things have been created through him and for him" (Col. 1:16).

✦ So Why Does This Matter? (Four Reasons) ✦

I can't possibly share all there is to know about God in a single intro to a single book. My library is filled with volume after volume of books written by scholars and pastors from throughout church history. And that's just one small sliver of the books written about God in a small library in one part of the world. The truth is we are like the apostle John, who, when finishing his gospel said, "And there are also many other things that Jesus did, which, if every one of them were written down, I suppose not even the world itself could contain the books that would be written" (John 21:25). The apostle Paul, one of the most learned Jewish minds of his day, threw up his hands and basically said, "Who has known the mind of the Lord?" (Rom. 11:34). Even the foremost Bible scholars, those whose lifelong pursuit fills the pages of the most prestigious academic journals, are but scratching the surface. We are like a child who walks a pace up Mount Everest, thinking he's scaled the entire summit.

And yet it does matter what we think about God. A. W. Tozer famously said that "what comes into our minds when we think about God is the most important thing about us."[11] And so, approaching this study of the creation story should cause us to reflect on the mighty truths we can grasp. John Walton writes of this importance: "Fallen human nature inevitably adopts a diluted, diminished, and in other ways corrupted concept of deity. Just as the Israelites had difficulty rising above the common view in their world that portrayed gods with needs and whims, so it is also difficult for us to rise above the common views of our world. Our world does not reduce God by distributing his power to other deities. Rather, we reduce God by making him a figurehead."[12]

As we approach the characters of creation, I'd like to offer four important realities that creation reveals about God and why they matter:

Creation reveals a God who is not like us. In the beginning, God reveals a God who is not a created being, a figment of our imaginations, a durable crutch we invent in difficult times. Genesis reveals an all-powerful God without beginning and end, who is other than His creation, who created something out of nothing.

I don't know about you, but this gives me comfort in a world gone mad. To know that there is a God who is above the messiness of this world and yet is driving history toward a conclusion. I find it comforting to know someone besides me is in charge, that I'm not the master of my fate, the captain of my soul. American religion is funny in that we act like we want a God we can reduce to our size, a God who overlooks our flaws and blesses our indiscretions. We want a God we can shape and shift. But is this really what we want? A God who is limited by our limitations, a God who is subject to our fears and captive to our whims? When we whisper those desperate prayers in the night, when we plead with God at the bedside of a loved one, when we pray over our children, we are praying to a God we need to be bigger than we are.

> When we plead with God at the bedside of a loved one, when we pray over our children, we are praying to a God we need to be bigger than we are.

A big God, a God I can't understand, a God I see with a holy awe, is a God whom I can trust is managing a world I cannot control, a God who can uphold the universe as I lay my head on my pillow and as I send my children out into the world and as I huddle in the darkness during a violent storm. Down deep in our souls, we don't want the cheap plastic gods of our age, but an all-powerful God who is bigger than the problems we face and can defeat the things that haunt us.

Creation reveals a God of order and beauty. Too often when we read Genesis, we read it as a kind of didactic dictionary, instead of stepping back and beholding, admiring, witnessing the way God has ordered the world. I like the way Old Testament scholar Sandra Richter, borrowing from Augustine and others, helps us see the intentional parallels of the days of creation:

- Day 1 introduces the creation of day and night, and Day 4 is the sun and moon to fill and rule them.
- Day 2 features the waters above and the waters below, and Day 5 features the birds and the fish to fill and rule them.
- Day 3 features the land and vegetation, and Day 6 features land mammals to fill and rule them.

Ruling over these three spheres of creation are God's unique creatures, fashioned in His image. Humans were given rule over the entire earth (Gen. 1:26). But humans ultimately rule under the Lordship and rule of God, who occupies the seventh day and rests.

The point of this scheme is to show us that God is not a God of chaos or division, but a God of beauty, unity, and order. God beheld all His creative acts and at each interval said, "This is good." It was only when humans, acting on their own volition and tempted by the serpent, tried to usurp the Lord of creation and thus were thrust from the garden (more on that later). So the world in which we live is one with less order and less beauty.

Creation reveals a God who is personal. Genesis describes a God who didn't just fashion the world and leave it alone, but who wants to be known. God is not distant. He speaks and is a Creator who made people for fellowship with Him and who is seen walking in perfect communion with Adam and Eve, who is ultimately revealed to us in the person of Jesus. There is a God who cries out, "Those who search for me will find me" (Prov. 8:17). He is a Father who sent His Son to be rejected and raised up on a Roman cross so that we could be reconciled to the One who made us. Softly and tenderly, the hymn writer reminds us, Jesus is calling for you.

This is ultimately the aim of this book, to help you know and be known by God; to stir in your heart affections for the One who made you. God can be very hard to see in a world gone mad, in a culture that increasingly punishes and shames and exploits, a world where it seems impossible to find comfort, even in those we love and treasure like family and friends, even in the small comforts of material things. But here is the comfort: God is *for* us. We can know and see, like David, that God is our "refuge and strength, a helper who is always found in times of trouble" (Ps. 46:1).

Creation reveals a God of the beginning and the end. To the prophet Isaiah, God declares, "See, I am doing a new thing!" (Isa. 43:19 NIV). Genesis doesn't just tell us how the world began, but how the world will end. The very phrase "In the beginning, God" tells us there will be an end. Beginnings are only beginnings because they have endings. And so we can open the first pages of our Bibles and see that God is already pointing us toward the end. The God of creation is the God of the new creation. In a sense, Genesis helps us read the rest of our Bibles. One scholar says, "If we possessed a Bible without Genesis, we would have a 'house of cards' without foundation or mortar. We cannot insure the continuing fruit of our spiritual heritage if we do not give place to its roots."[13]

Understanding Genesis will then help you see that some of the most recognizable features of Eden show up throughout the rest of Scripture. Consider a few examples. The river that runs through the garden shows up in the vision of heaven we find in Psalm 46: "There is a river whose streams make glad the city of God," and ultimately in Revelation, where John's vision describes the New Jerusalem. The tree of life from Eden becomes a disfigured and cursed cross upon which the Son of God offers life to those who believe and then shows up in the New Jerusalem as a source of health and life (Rev. 22:2). Eden is a temple, where God dwells in harmony with His people. A relationship broken by sin would then be mediated by lesser temples throughout the story of Israel and then be restored by Jesus through the indwelling Spirit of God in the new temple of redeemed sinners, and ultimately in perfect fellowship as God dwells with His people in the restored city of God.[14]

Sandra Richter writes that "everything that lies in between Eden's gate and the New Jerusalem, the bulk of our Bibles, is in essence a huge rescue plan. In fact, we could summarize the plot line of the Bible into one cosmic question: 'How do we get Adam back into the garden? In Genesis 3, humanity was driven out; in Revelation 21–22, they are welcomed home.'"[15]

Welcomed home! What a wonderful thought as we embark on this journey together. I invite you to drink deeply in the creation story, as we look at characters like Adam and Eve, Cain and Abel, Noah and his sons, as well as that evil serpent who deceives, and the strange characters like the mysterious *Nephilim*, among others. The point is not another exercise in knowing useless trivia, but to drink deeply from the fountain of God's Word, to know and understand more about God, about ourselves, and about our world, and ultimately, to join with the rest of creation in worshiping our great God.

> *The morning stars sang together and all the sons of God shouted for joy. (Job 38:7)*

CHAPTER ONE

The Delinquent

Adam, First, Fallen, and Forgiven

*The two decisive figures in human history are Adam and Christ.
Adam brought into the world the great enemies of human
happiness—sin and death. These twin powers reign over all those
in Adam and only those in Christ conquer sin and death and
become righteous and live.*[1]

—TOM SCHREINER

Some nights, I sit up and thank the Lord Jesus for the next breath."
These words whispered to me from a dear friend who struggled
with COVID for many months. Most of us don't spend our moments
thinking about the next time we inhale oxygen and exhale carbon di-
oxide, we don't ponder for a second every expansion and contraction of
our lungs. We just breathe, because breathing is natural, subconscious.

But a global pandemic made us think about breathing in a way
we hadn't thought about it before, from the way our exhaling often
carries germs and viruses to others, to the way so many languished
in hospitals connected to ventilators, laboring for each breath, to the
millions around the world who tragically perished from COVID-19,
unable to take another breath on their own.

Imagine with me, then, the very first breath from the very first human who walked the face of the earth. Genesis describes it this way: "Then the LORD God formed the man out of the dust from the ground and breathed the breath of life into his nostrils, and the man became a living being" (Gen. 2:7). The first breath was a breath of God into the lungs of the very first human.

This tells us something about how God thinks about human beings. Consider the care with which Moses describes Adam's creation. Every other creature God spoke into existence, but the human race, Moses writes, was carefully crafted from the dust of the ground.

God created Adam with such thoughtfulness. *Let us make man* implies a conference among the Godhead—Father, Son, and Spirit. Consider the use of vivid language describing God, the grand artist forming and shaping Adam with His hands and breathing into Adam the breath of life, a process King David would later elaborate on in vivid detail, the care with which every human soul is fashioned by the Creator. "You knit me together in my mother's womb," we read in Psalm 139. Francis Schaeffer says of Genesis, "It is as though God put exclamation points here to indicate that there is something special about the creation of man."[2]

There *is* something special. Genesis pulsates with the beauty and mystery of the origins of human life, so much so that Moses is telling us that the apex of God's creative acts is the creature on whom He stamped His image. Eden is incomplete without human life: *there was no man to work the ground*, Moses emphasizes, as if to say that the earth, in all of its majestic splendor, is lifeless without the human race to cultivate it as God's image-bearers.

Humans, unlike any part of creation, bear the *imago Dei*, the image of God. What does this mean? The best minds, throughout the ages, have pondered this topic, but ultimately we can say that to be made in the image of God means that in some way Adam—and every human being since—reflects God. This implies both responsibility—we are not our own and were created for God's glory—as well as a certain dignity. This chapter doesn't give me sufficient space to flesh out the massive implications of this core Christian teaching. But this is how I defined it in my book *The Dignity Revolution*:

> So what exactly does it mean to be created "in the image of God"? It means both that we are not God and also that we are not animals or angels. To acknowledge the fact that we are made in his image means embracing both humility and enjoying dignity.
>
> Our dignity flows from and is rooted in the truth that we are like God. You are more than simply the sum of your parts. You are not merely a highly evolved mammal. You are not just a collection of atoms. You are not just what others see or the combination of others' verdicts on you. . . .
>
> Our humility grows in the soil of the truth that we are not God. You are not the center of your own universe, the master of your own fate. You are not the arbiter of right and wrong. You cannot find sufficient reason for your existence or fulfillment in your existence from within.[3]

We are not the sum of our parts. We are not random. This is good news in a world increasingly asking the question about what it means to be human. The opening pages of our Bible give us a most profound and beautiful definition. Genesis is here to tell us that human beings are not here merely by accident or chance, but that Adam and every single person was created with intentionality and purpose by a loving Father.

Let's pause and think about this for a moment. In a world where human life seems so cheap, where people are stalked and abused and killed, where tyrannical governments commit atrocities, where terrorists indiscriminately murder innocents, where ideologies spanning the spectrum fight to elevate one ethnic group at the expense of another, the Word of God declares with boldness that human beings are precious and valuable.

Moses is telling us here that Adam was not created merely as yet another of the magnificent creatures God spoke into existence, but was formed and shaped from dust as a special creation of God, given breath and life and "crowned [with] glory and honor" (Ps. 8:5). James Montgomery Boice stated it well: "Here lies our true worth. We are made in God's image and are therefore valuable to God and others. God loves men and women, as he does not and cannot love the animals, plants, or inanimate matter."[4] I don't know what you are doing right now as you read that last quote from Boice, but I hope you are letting it sink in. You have value! Your neighbor has value! And yes, that eccentric friend on Facebook has value!

Fourth-century church father John Chrysostom reads Genesis and declares: "It is humanity, the greatest and most marvelous of living beings, and the creation most worthy of honor before God."[5] Humans, the greatest and most marvelous of living beings. You may have woken up today not feeling so great and marvelous. But you are.

I can't emphasize enough how vital this truth is to understanding the Bible and to understanding our world. This theology should shape the way God's people think both about their own worth and value and how we think about the worth and value of other image-bearers. There are no mere human beings. Those people at the office with whom you disagree, that crazy uncle who spouts off at Thanksgiving, that politician whose policies you despise—each and every one is an image-bearer of God. In a sense, understanding the *imago Dei* should humble us. We are but mere particles of dust given life by the breath of the Almighty (Ps. 103:14 says, "he knows what we are made of, remembering that we are dust"), and yet we are so much more. We are reflections of the divine.

✦ Was Adam Real? ✦

But let's think about what it was like to be Adam. Before we can do that, we must deal with the elephant in the room. Do we really believe Adam was a real person or is he just a kind of figurehead, a symbol illustrating the concepts of creation and the fall and the preciousness of human life? There is quite a debate among Bible scholars. Many find the idea of a real Adam hard to square with modern science.[6]

However, I find it hard to read the rest of Scripture and come away with the idea that Adam was a mere figurehead or myth. For one thing, Moses and other Old Testament writers, under the inspiration of the Holy Spirit, write as if Adam was a real person, both describing his behavior and actions, but also listing him in genealogies as if he was a real human being and not a mythical figure. And when you get to the New Testament, you find Jesus and Paul both assume Adam is a real person.

Jesus, referring to Genesis in a question from the Pharisees, responded:

> *"Haven't you read," he replied, "that he who created them in the beginning made them male and female and he also said, 'For this reason a man will leave his father and mother and be joined to his*

*wife, and the two will become one flesh'? So they are no longer two,
but one flesh. Therefore, what God has joined together, let no one
separate." (Matt. 19:4–6)*

Jesus preached from Genesis as if the narrative in Genesis was true.
I think we are on dangerous ground if we, in the twenty-first century,
presume to know more than Jesus knew! And then there is Paul, one
of the foremost Hebrew scholars of his day, trained under the great
Hebrew teacher Gamaliel, and inspired by the Spirit of God to write
much of the New Testament. Paul didn't hesitate to point to Adam as
the very first human whose sin plunged humanity into darkness. Paul
referred to Adam multiple times in his New Testament letters (Acts
17; Rom. 5; 1 Cor. 15; 1 Tim. 2). To a pagan audience, Paul declared,
"From *one man*, he has made every nationality to live over the whole
earth and has determined their appointed times and the boundaries
of where they live" (Acts 17:16). Theologian Millard Erickson writes,
"not only did the New Testament writers like Paul believe that an
actual Adam and Eve existed, but it was an indispensable part of their
doctrine of humanity."[7]

For most of church history, Christians have debated specifics on
the age of the Earth or the details of the process of creation described
in Genesis. But a literal Adam is essential for the central storyline of
Scripture to hold together. Scholar Philip Ryken writes why this is important: "To deny the historical Adam is to stand against the teaching
of Moses, Luke, Jesus and Paul . . . Given his recurring presence in the
biblical narrative, the logical and long-term effect of denying the existence of Adam is to weaken the church's grip on central biblical truths
that make a difference in daily life."[8]

Perhaps you find the idea of humans originating from one central figure named Adam a bit far-fetched. Some Christians have found ways to reconcile a belief in Adam as a myth with a faithful reading of Scripture. But I can't do that. What's more, I don't find it impossible that God could create the human race from one single person, a special creation at a specific time and place. After all, I believe even more scientifically implausible things, like a man getting swallowed by a great fish, a body of water being divided so a nation can cross, and, the most implausible of all, that a man from Nazareth was both God and man who was killed by Romans and then walked out of a rich man's tomb three days later. Yes, I believe all of those things.

I think this plain reading of Genesis is not only the right way to read our Bibles but has profound implications for how we see our world. It is a radical idea that every single person on this earth, regardless of their ethnicity, their social status, their family heritage, was both created in the image of God and also draws from the same family tree. Understanding Genesis helps us see our neighbors the way God sees them, helps us build bridges across racial and socioeconomic lines, helps us resist the evil prejudices that so tempt every generation of fallen humanity. We live in a world laden with perverse incentives to divide along racial, social, economic, and political lines. We are daily tempted with rich opportunities to see other people as less than human.

This is why I believe so strongly in the truth as we see it in Genesis, why I chose to write this book in the first place, and why I think it's important to understand who Adam is.

Adam, as the very first human to walk the earth, experienced a supernatural kind of birth and was created to live out a calling unlike any other human being in history. He was alone in the world, born with no history and no parents. Every other person born would have come from another person—by birth. Even his wife, Eve, was created from Adam's rib. But Adam was formed from the dust of the ground by God's hands.

Imagine that. Each of us first opens our eyes to the world when we are born; gradually, we grow and mature. There is nothing I delight in more than seeing my children grow up before my very eyes. But for Adam, his was a unique kind of existence. He had no earthly mother or father to guide him, no template of experiences passed down through history. Can you imagine what his first moments of reality must have been like, imagine that first breath? His first thoughts? His first time using his eyes to behold the beauty of Eden and his mouth to communicate with the Creator? What was it like to be "walking in the garden in the cool of the day" with God (Gen. 3:8 kjv)?

Adam was the first, but his would not be the last miraculous birth, born for a special God-given purpose. Isaac was born to a couple whose childbearing years were long in their rearview mirror, born to birth a people and a nation out of whom the Messiah would come. Samuel, a prophet, priest, and judge in Israel, was conceived in the womb of Hannah, whose faithful prayers for a child reached heaven. John the Baptist was born to an aging priest who doubted the word of the angel who promised his wife would give birth to a prophet, one whose life would pave the way for the coming of Jesus. And of course, Jesus, called the second Adam by the apostle Paul in Corinthians and Romans, whose birth was not only supernatural but also conceived by the Holy Spirit in the womb of a common peasant girl. In a way, God's breathing of life and creating Adam from dust foreshadows the breath of new creation God would breathe into His new people through the power of the Holy Spirit, in the salvation that Jesus would bring by His life, death, and resurrection.

In a sense, every one of us is the product of a supernatural birth. Every birth, King David reminds us in Psalm 139, is the product of God's careful handiwork and every spiritual birth is the result of the miraculous power of the Holy Spirit and the sacrifice of Jesus on the cross.

✦ Born to Build ✦

Not only was Adam created in a special way, he was created for a special purpose. The narrative in Genesis moves quickly from Adam's unique creation to Adam's unique calling:

> *God blessed them, and God said to them, "Be fruitful, multiply, fill the earth, and subdue it. Rule the fish of the sea, the birds of the sky, and every creature that crawls on the earth." (Gen. 1:28)*

Subdue. Rule. These commands were first given to Adam to cultivate Eden, but it is the obligation of every image-bearer. We know this because even after the fall, after God punished the world with a great flood (more on that later), God urged Noah (Gen. 9) to cultivate creation. Creating, building, working, and resting are the primary ways humans represent God in the world. Listen again to Genesis:

> *The LORD God took the man and placed him in the garden of Eden to work it and watch over it. (Gen. 2:15)*

To work it and watch over it. Eden was a blank canvas given to humans by God for their creativity and His glory. Work is not a punishment brought on by the curse of sin, but a gift, a way we worship the God whose image we bear.

Humans were given stewardship of God's world. Adam was given the task of naming the animals, a seemingly never-ending job in a world teeming with unlimited expressions of God's creativity. The job of naming wasn't God merely delegating on a busy day. It is God bestowing on His image-bearers the gift to care for creation. To name is to have authority. Notice throughout Scripture, God's naming: renaming Abram to Abraham, renaming Simon to Peter, Saul to Paul and ultimately Jesus, who is given a "name that is above every name" (Phil. 2:9).

Understanding this mandate, this authority to rule, should shape the way we see our world. We are keepers of creation and not its creator. Adam's sin and our sin is a both a rejection of God's rule and an abdication of our rulership over creation. The mere act of listening to the lying words of a serpent is Adam subjecting himself to an animal kingdom over which he was made to rule.

> Work is not a punishment brought on by the curse of sin, but a gift, a way we worship the God whose image we bear.

This side of Adam's fall, we fail to obey our mandate to rule and cultivate in two ways. Humans are tempted to exploit rather than cultivate God's creation, neglecting our role as the stewards of God's world. Or we embrace the tendency to worship the earth in ways that sets us up against our Creator. This is evident in much of the language today around environmentalism and climate change, which at times seems to assume that humans possess total power over the universe, instead of God, who is "sustaining all things by his powerful word" (Heb. 1:3). Earth worship instead of worship of the Creator leads to policies that often hurt the people for whom the earth was created: human beings. Obeying Genesis means resisting both a throwaway attitude of increasing consumption that ignores the care of natural resources and a godless green religion that pits the earth against the creatures for which it was created.

Ultimately now, in a fallen world, our work to cultivate is made more difficult as the ground fights back. Embedded in the curse pronounced by God as a result of Adam's sin, our work is fraught with difficulty, thorns and thistles fighting back in the gardens of life. And yet the work we do, even the work that seems unworthy, is a way we glorify the One who gave us work as a gift.

God's instructions to Adam should also shape our view of technology. On one hand, we can easily worship progress as a kind of minigod, with every new piece of technology as a kind of object of worship, with every new Apple event a kind of secular temple and inventors like Elon Musk our mini-gods. We're tempted to put our faith in "science," that kind of catch-all term for observable and man-made discovery that easily forgets the One who created the raw materials and left them for us to discover in the first place.

We can also be pulled away from technology in a way that almost worships the simple and the rural, as if an untouched Eden is the ultimate end for the people of God. The narrative of Scripture doesn't point us backward to a remembered "good old days," but forward to a future, restored New Jerusalem, and a second Adam who fulfills the mandate that the first Adam failed. Eden, undeveloped and raw, is not where we are headed. Heaven, a city, is our destiny. Genesis points forward to Revelation.

So we should ask questions about our technology, in a world where it can be corrupted and have evil ends, while also championing new advances that are signs of our fulfillment of the creation mandate. And yet we should recognize that God's new creation people are a forward-looking people. The writer of Hebrews describes faithful Christians as people who are "looking forward to the city . . . whose architect and builder is God" (Heb. 11:10).

✦ As in Adam ✦

So she took some of its fruit and ate it; she also gave some to her husband, who was with her, and he ate it. (Gen. 3:6)

And he ate it. And in that moment—however long it takes to bite into a piece of fruit—the world was forever changed. Created in innocence, surrounded by an idyllic creation, enjoying intimacy with a beautiful wife, and experiencing perfect communion with God, Adam threw it all away.

I find it interesting that while God pronounces a curse on Adam *and* Eve, most of the Bible's judgment comes for Adam. It is Adam who is banished from the garden, and Adam that God goes calling after. Clearly sin impacted both Adam and Eve, but though Eve was first to eat the forbidden fruit, it is Adam upon whom responsibility rests for humanity's descent into darkness. In Romans 5 and 1 Corinthians 15, Paul uses the phrase "by one man" and "as in Adam" as the starting point of sin's entrance into the world.

We too often think of the fall in the garden of Eden as only a story of a woman being duped by a snake. But the Bible tells us that there is much more going on here. I find it interesting that Scripture places responsibility for the initial sin—the sin that lit the match that set the world on fire—on the shoulders of Adam, whose actions, we are told, have ushered death into the world (1 Cor. 15:22). While the curse pronounced to Eve is significant—childbirth marked by struggle and pain and often death, and a world in which men would often take advantage of their superior status in society's hierarchy—the bulk of the curse seems to fall on Adam's shoulders. It was Adam, after all, who was created first. It was Adam who was given initial responsibility for the garden. It was Adam who abdicated his role as protector of Eve and steward of God's good creation.

In the modern era it is quite controversial to consider this arranging of roles. It almost strikes us as sexist for the Bible to put the blame mostly on Adam's shoulders, as if Eve had no agency. But rather than disempowering women, it is pointing toward a kind of servant leadership required of Adam and every husband to lead in a way that protects the bodies and souls of those God has put under our care.

Adam allowed his wife to be poisoned by the rhetorical bite of the snake. It was Adam who didn't proactively fight off the snake, declaring God's promises over and against the lies of the enemy, but instead nodded his head and agreed with the lies of Satan against the One who created him. It was Adam who should have used his God-given authority over the animal kingdom to resist the serpent.

Now, in an instant, Adam's entire existence was changed, and not for the better. In an instant, he was separated from the God who knelt in the dust and formed him with such care. In an instant, his relationship with his wife went from harmony to discord, from mutual love and sharing to blame shifting and resentment. *The woman you gave to be with me. . .* his bitterness spills out.

And this one action didn't just ruin Adam's life; it distorted the lives of every single person who would ever live. The eating of that piece of fruit soured God's good creation, twisted the human experience, and like a tsunami, brought waves of sin and death into the world.

If you want to know why the world is messed up, why the oceans rise, why tornadoes strike, why volcanoes erupt, why hurricanes ravage the coasts, look no further than this crime scene in Genesis 3. If you want to understand why young people are gunned down on our city streets, why tyrants like Hitler and Pol Pot put millions of civilians in the grave, why governments could buy and sell human flesh as property, glance backward at a naked couple, a rotten apple, and a hissing serpent. If you seek the truth about our human condition, why even the best of us have dark demons we hide from the world, why addictions ravage us against our best efforts, why we try and fail to love, don't miss the stark truth from the opening pages of your Bible.

You can find other stories that try to explain the world as it is, but only this narrative offers a mirror to our true selves. The world is on fire because a poison called sin slithered into the garden and poisoned the world God made. To quote the late R. C. Sproul, "we are not sinners because we sin, we sin because we are sinners."[9] Every person who enters this world enters with a moral defect, a condition that can't be cured by behavior modification, religion, or even medicine.

Of course, we read Genesis 3 and it seems so easy in hindsight, doesn't it? *Adam, you were given a beautiful garden, a beautiful wife, everything you need. Just don't eat the wrong thing.* Yet it wasn't just Adam and Eve and a serpent there that day. I was there too, standing guilty with disobedience on my hands. When Adam sinned, we sinned. My sins contribute to the brokenness and devastation of our world. Your sins contribute to the brokenness and devastation of our world. We are what's wrong in the world.

And yet Genesis 3 isn't the end of the story the Bible tells. Even in God's pronouncement of the curse, he hints at hope, offers echoes of resurrection. A violent clash between Adam's offspring and the serpent would unfold in history in this sin-addled world, but a new Adam would arise to clean up our mess:

> *For if by the one man's trespass the many died, how much more have the grace of God and the gift which comes through the grace of the one man Jesus Christ overflowed to the many . . . For just as through one man's disobedience the many were made sinners, so also through the one man's obedience the many will be made righteous.*
> *(Rom. 5:15–19)*

> *For since death came through a man, the resurrection of the dead also comes through a man. For just as in Adam all die, so also in Christ all will be made alive. (1 Cor. 15:21–22)*

There would be another garden. And this time a second Adam would not stand idly by but would accept God's cup of divine wrath. The first Adam didn't have the last word. The innocent one would climb a tree of death to rescue those separated from the tree of life. He would reverse the curse of sin and offer a new kind of fruit, not forbidden, but one born of the grace God now offers to Adam, Eve and their ancestors. New Testament scholar Tom Schreiner writes:

> Adam's influence in the world was exclusively negative in that he brought death and devastation into the cosmos. Jesus Christ, by bringing life and by triumphing over sin, counteracted and reversed

the downward pull of Adam's sin . . . sin reigns in the domain of death through Adam, but now grace also reigns, and the result is eternal life through the saving righteousness of Jesus Christ . . . Grace is so powerful that it cleans up the mess produced by Adam and produces the wholeness God intended in creating human beings in the first place.[10]

It's hard to see this through the dirty porthole through which we view the world. Standing in Eden's aftermath, we can only lament what our first family did to usher in sin and death. We can only see sorrow and guilt from our own unrighteous actions before God. And yet there is good news that on the horizon, a Savior awaits.

The first Adam didn't have the last word.

Grace cleans up Adam's mess. Grace cleans up our mess.

✦ Naked and Afraid ✦

Imagine Adam. Imagine the surreal whiplash he experienced in those moments after the fall. He and Eve went from being naked and unafraid to totally exposed before the God of the universe, to a level of knowledge and experience that only ever brought pain. In a moment he saw it all come to an end. Imagine the weight of guilt in his heart at what he had wrought.

Imagine the regret he would feel as he watched his sons and daughters inflicted by the consequences of his own actions. How he would long, in the hundreds of years he would live beyond this day, for those good old days. How he would replay in his mind the conversations with the serpent. How he would beat himself up for his sins.

But there was no escape, no hiding, no retreat from where he was now. None of us can imagine what it was like, what it must have been like, to be Adam. We can't know what it would be like to wake up in Eden and to be kicked out by God's fiery angels.

And yet we do know what it's like to carry around guilt. Like Adam, we look back longingly what we've lost: the bad decisions, the failed relationships, the sins we've indulged. We see the widening chasm between what we should be and who we really are. We lie awake at night and replay our lives and lament the fallout of our sins on our kids, our neighbors, our friends. We ache and long for that home, for those good old days, for a relationship with our Creator.

You wonder how Adam bore this weight. He lived over 900 years, centuries of his sin compounding in misery, to generation upon generation. He'd suffer the tragedy of seeing one son rise up in hatred and murder another son. Imagine at that funeral, Adam in anguish, wishing he could go back to that fateful day in Eden when he'd passively acquiesced to rebellion. God had said that death would come, but could he have imagined he'd be staring at the lifeless body of his own son?

And yet Adam could cling to the faint glimmer of hope that one would come who could bear the weight of Adam's guilt and your guilt. God would visit, in a Son born of a daughter of Eve. He who, unlike Adam, knew no sin, would become sin for Adam (2 Cor. 5:21), for me and for all who call Him Lord. The Lord would lay on this second Adam the sin of us all (Isa. 53:6).

Adam, standing in the ashes of a world to which he had set fire, huddles, hidden in incomplete makeshift clothes. And yet he hears good news, the Father's haunting, searching words, "Where are you?" These words, says Derek Kidner, have "all the marks of grace."[11] Adam was caught red-handed by God. The God who sees all things saw Adam's teeth sink into that fruit. "No creature is hidden from his sight, but all things are naked and exposed to the eyes of him to whom we must give account," the writer of Hebrews reminds us, as if we didn't already know, subconsciously, that we are not alone from God.

Naked and exposed was Adam. Imagine the most embarrassing, humiliating, shaming moment of your life and here was Adam's dilemma. Those hidden sins, those dark spots you buried in your heart that nobody knows. Well, God sees. God sees you. He knows the real Adam, the real you.

And yet, a comfort. "Where are you?" was not a bewildered God, looking for a lost child. "Where are you?" is a grieving Father pursuing a wayward son. "Where are you?" is the aging patriarch in Jesus' story of the prodigal, lifting up his garments and sprinting toward his beloved. "Where are you?" is the Good Shepherd, leaving the ninety-nine sheep and going after the lost lamb.

"Where are you?" is the entire Christian story, God seeking and saving those who have deliberately disobeyed him. It's a radical, otherworldly, almost ridiculous love. This is why God sent His only begotten to bleed on a cruel Roman cross.

Today, God is still whispering, "Where are you?" I've heard the distant whisper of God as I made my way up the hot and dusty aisle at youth camp, while another verse of "Just As I Am" played. Others have heard Jesus say, "Where are you?" at the end of bottle of whiskey, their last measure of self-will erased by impossibility. Still others have listened to the distant call of "Where are you?" while searching history in vain for ways to explain away the miraculous.

We've heard "Where are you?" as we've sat in the reality of our own sin. We've heard "Where are you?" as we've gazed up at the nail-pierced hands of the One who never bit the fruit, who never yielded to the temptations of the serpent, who instead poured out His life for me.

"Where are you?" is the entire Christian story.

"We see ourselves in the Garden, hearing the Lord call 'Where are you?' We know what it is to hide through shame. We are skilled at shifting blame on to others. We feel the cost of being expelled from Eden. . . . We are part of the story. We are there in the Garden and the Word is addressed to us,"[12] writes David Atkinson.

Maybe you are, while reading this book, standing like Adam in the wake of your own mess. Maybe you are naked and exposed, crushed under the weight of your sins. I hope in these pages you can hear the distant call, the cry from Eden to Nazareth to Calvary, of the One who is calling you, beckoning you to look up, to come home. Genesis 3 doesn't have to be the end of your story. God seeks you in your despair, having sent Jesus to take on the weight of sin while we were "still sinners" (Rom. 5:8).

This is the real story of Genesis. The story begins with Adam's first breath, breathed into his nostrils by the Creator, winds its way through the story of Israel, as the same Spirit that breathed on the waters in creation is promised by the prophets (Ezek. 37; Joel 2) to come and breath new life into a new people. On a cruel Roman cross, the second Adam would breathe His last breath (Mark 15:37) so that we could be saved, and yet would shake off death, rising again to breathe new life into those who believe (John 20:22).

I want you to find joy in this reality as you leave this chapter. I want you to look around at a world so broken by sin and recognize that this world is not as it should be, but that Jesus Christ is renewing and restoring and will one day make all things new, including our own souls if we reject the way of our first Adam and pledge allegiance to the second. I leave you with the words of Charles Wesley in a famous Christmas hymn:

> Come, desire of nations, come,
> Fix in us thy humble home!
> Rise, the woman's conquering seed,
> Bruise in us the serpent's head!
>
> .   .   .   .
>
> Adam's likeness, Lord, efface;
> Stamp thy image in its place;
> Second Adam from above,
> Reinstate us in thy love![13]

CHAPTER TWO

The Forbidden

Eve, the Misled Mother of All

*Just as the rib is found at the side of the man and is attached to him,
even so the good wife, the rib of her husband, stands at his side
to be his helper-counterpart, and her soul is bound up with his.*[1]

—UMBERTO CASSUTO

We live a contradiction. More connected than any people in history, we are so lonely. Right now I can hardly keep my eyes on the laptop and away from my iPhone, alive with texts from friends and coworkers. If I so desire (and I so desire), I can quickly switch apps and get that dopamine-delivering experience of seeing people in my mentions on Twitter or comments on Facebook. I may venture over to Instagram and see that delightful bubble tell me someone just commented. The anticipation kills me. When I'm bored, I can dial up friends in multiple states, FaceTime my parents or siblings, or check my email.

On the one hand, it's wonderful to live in the digital age. I can reach almost anyone. I can text my kids terrible dad jokes. I can meet interesting people online and learn and grow from others I may have never discovered in another age. At the same time, aren't we all feeling an increasing sense of being disconnected?

Online communities offer some measure of togetherness, but are they really a substitute for genuine embodied friendship? This is why we are fracturing as a society, sorting ourselves into angry tribes, the institutions that hold diverse people together fraying at the edges. This kind of connected loneliness is why one social commentator observes an ominous sign:

> A nation of increasingly lonely, friendless citizens given outlets to find collective, communal fulfillment online will be a nation spawning a range of radical political factions, groups, or movements defined by and drawing the bulk of their cohesion from their loathing of other factions, groups, or movements.[2]

Of course, the global pandemic that radically upended our social lives exacerbated this trend and, perhaps, helped us see how damaging it is for us to be alone. Perhaps it's time to recover the truth about how humans were created, a truth echoed in the ancient words of the very first book of the Bible. Moses, writing with the whisper of the Spirit, chronicling creation as the words of God Himself, stops to record the Creator:

> *Then the LORD God said, "It is not good for the man to be alone. I will make a helper corresponding to him." (Gen. 2:18)*

Moses slows down just enough for us to catch a glimpse of what he is trying to say. An entire story pulsating with frequent commentary on the goodness of God's creation. The original Artist, stepping back from his handiwork to emphatically say: "Ahh yes, this right here is good, very good." Well . . . except for one moment where God pauses and declares, "This, though, is not very good." What was not good? What was the catalyst for this profound social commentary by the Almighty?

God wanted all of creation, all of heaven, all of history to know that it is not good at all for humans to live alone without other humans. It's amazing that we modern people, so proud of our sophistication and science and forward thinking, are coming around to an axiom buried in God's natural way of doing things. Humans were made for each other. Made to not be alone.[3]

✦ Waking Up Eve ✦

How long was Adam alone? How long between the first flicker of his eyes and the times those eyes first saw the wife God had created for him? The Bible doesn't tell us this, but reading Genesis gives us the sense that perhaps Adam had more than a few lonely days and nights.

It is into this desperation, this gap in God's creative work, that the very first woman was formed by the hand of God. Eve was created to answer the need for human connection.

A unique and special creation as supernatural and awe-inspiring as Adam's, Eve has been the source of speculation and curiosity from the beginning. God could have created Eve from anything. After all, making stuff with little material, with no material, with mere words is not a problem for God.

Yet God fashions Eve from Adam, a sign human life would always be interconnected and interdependent, that male and female, distinct and different, are so much alike. God puts Adam into a deep coma. Did Adam take a nap after a long day of animal naming? Was he made drowsy by a special plant with melatonin-like effects? Did he hit his head? We don't know. We do know that God deliberately caused the first man to fall into a deep sleep, pain-free enough to perform the very first invasive surgery, removing a rib from Adam's side and creating a stunningly beautiful human being so much like Adam and yet so different. "Not made out of his head to top him, not out of his feet to be trampled upon by him, but out of his side to be equal with him, under his arm to be protected, and near his heart to be beloved,"[4] says seventeenth-century British pastor Matthew Henry.

So much mystery here. God, who breathed the first breath into Adam, begins with the very bone and sinew that protects that breath and weaves together the first female. In this, a sign of Calvary's sacrifice. Adam, John Calvin writes, "lost . . . one of his ribs; but instead of it, a far richer reward was granted him, since he obtained a faithful associate of life; for he now saw himself, who had before been imperfect; rendered complete in his wife. And in this we see a true resemblance of our union with the Son of God; for he became weak that he might have members of his body endued with strength."[5]

Imagine reading this book of origins as a Jewish person living in the land of Canaan, among the pagans whose view of women was so misogynistic that they saw women as mere material for the satisfaction and pleasure of powerful men. It's a countercultural tale Moses is telling, in which the very first woman was made with the same level of care, the same level of intentionality, the same level of awe-inspiring creativity as the man. Made of the same stuff, given the same breath of God, stamped with the same *imago Dei.* John Milton, in *Paradise Lost* says:

> O fairest of creation, last and best
> Of all God's works, creature in whom excelled
> Whatever can to sight or thought be formed,
> Holy, divine, good, amiable, or sweet![6]

Eve's creation means creation is now complete. Men and women, together, a full reflection of the divine. Mary Kassian describes this coming together of male and female: "Though both sexes bear God's image fully on their own, each does so in a unique and distinct way."[7]

We don't have to imagine Adam's response to the first sight of Eve. Adam is quite pleased with the woman God has created, so pleased he writes a poem (putting every other male afterward to shame in our lame attempts at romance). Stirred from his sleep, shaking off the cobwebs of his coma, Adam opens his eyes and beholds. Here are the words that came out:

> *This one, at last, is bone of my bone*
> *and flesh of my flesh;*
> *this one will be called "woman,"*
> *for she was taken from man.*

At last. How long did Adam wait in silence and loneliness, counting creature after creature, wishing, hoping, wondering if there would be another like him? Derek Kidner says this "reveals him as a social being, made for fellowship, not power; he will not live until he loves, giving himself away to another on his own level. So the woman is presented wholly as his partner and counterpart. She is valued for herself alone."[8]

Eve's first breath, the first fluttering of her eyes in the world God created, was different than Adam's. Whereas Adam awoke as the first human, Eve entered the world with immediate companionship, with a world more ordered than when her husband was created by God. She entered life in intimacy with God and companionship with her beloved.

✦ Take and Eat ✦

The world that greeted Eve as she first experienced life was a world created by God for her pleasure and God's glory. We don't really know exactly where Eden was. Four rivers flow from Eden, two of which we recognize today. The Tigris River begins in the mountains of eastern Turkey and runs all the way along Turkey's border with Syria. The Euphrates begins in the Turkish Highlands and makes its way through Syria and Iraq, eventually dumping into the Persian Gulf. Two other rivers, Gihon and Pishon, are lost to us today.

We don't know where Eden was, but that could be by design. It seems as if God has intended for us not to know exactly where this special place is, for we might be tempted to vainly go back and reclaim what was lost, to reenter a place from which we were expelled. What we do know is Adam and Eve were placed in a special garden within Eden, into a lush and beautiful home where God dwelt, surrounded by unlimited natural resources and the presence of God Himself.

Eden is a garden, but it has all the features of a temple, the place where God dwells. In Eden, a cherubim guards the entrance, a feature we see later adorning the ark of the covenant. We see rivers, which are featured prominently in the prophet Ezekiel's vision of a restored temple and have a prominent place in the coming New Jerusalem. And Eden also features a tree of life, a symbol of immortality. This tree shows up at the end of the Bible, a prominent feature in the New Jerusalem. But it would take the second Adam ascending a tree of death for God's image-bearers to find full enjoyment with the tree of life.

We often focus on the forbidden fruit without seeing all that *wasn't* forbidden.

Old Testament scholar Sandra Richter writes of Eden:

> This was Adam and Eve's perfect world. Not just fruit and fig leaves, but an entire race of people stretching their cognitive and creative powers to the limit to build a society of balance and justice and joy. Here the sons of Adam and the daughters of Eve would learn life at the feet of the Father, build their city in the shadow of the Almighty, create and design and expand within the protective confines of his kingdom.[9]

It's hard for us to imagine how Eve could survey her life in Eden, in perfect intimacy with her husband Adam and perfect fellowship with her Creator, and still choose the way of the serpent. We often focus on the forbidden fruit—was it an apple, pomegranate, a pear?—without seeing all that *wasn't* forbidden. Notice how often Genesis 1 tells us how much God had given them: *I have given you every seed-bearing plant on the surface of the entire earth. I have given you every tree whose fruit contains seed. I have given you all the wildlife of the earth. Every bird of the sky. Every creature that crawls on the earth—everything having the breath of life—every green plant for food.*

And then repeated in Genesis 2, God says, *you are free to eat from any tree of the garden.* And listen to the whispers of the serpent, who pivoted Eve's focus away from everything she did have—plants, trees, wildlife, perfection union with her husband, intimacy with God—and toward what she didn't have: "Did God really say, 'You can't eat from any tree in the garden'?" the serpent asks, rhetorically. You can almost hear a murmured, mocking chuckle: *Can you believe this? Why won't God let you touch that tree?*

Hearing these words of doubt and suspicion, Eve would no longer see God as the good Father, who lovingly shaped her out of Adam's rib, who planted her in a luscious paradise, but as a stingy Father who is holding out on us. This is always how sin begins to have its way with us. Paul would later offer a searing indictment of Eve's choice:

> *For although they knew God, they did not honor him as God or give thanks to him, but they became futile in their thinking, and their foolish hearts were darkened. Claiming to be wise, they became fools, and exchanged the glory of the immortal God for images resembling mortal man and birds and animals and creeping things.* (Rom. 1:21–23 ESV)

We know these murmurings all too well, in a world broken after Eden. The enemy tells us that what we have is not enough. Your marriage isn't enough. Your career isn't enough. Your doctrine isn't enough. Ultimately, the enemy is telling us that God isn't enough. Because Adam and Even sinned, we live with this lie embedded in our hearts, embedded in the world around us, the advice that tells us to just follow our hearts, to throw off the shackles of God's good design. As a result, so many sons and daughters of Eve live enslaved to desire.

It seemed so frivolous, God's restrictions on Adam and Eve. You can almost hear yourself reading Genesis and whispering back to God, *C'mon God, just let them have the fruit.* What's the big deal? Why so stingy, so legalistic?

This is how we think today. Why is God so restrictive on sexuality? Why so narrow when it comes to greed? Why so specific when it comes to pathways to salvation?

And yet it was so much more than a piece of fruit. "The blessings are many, the stipulations few," writes Richter. "In fact, the only negative stipulation of this covenant is 'you shall not eat of the tree of the knowledge of good and evil.' On the surface this seems like a simple, even silly rule. But in reality this one edict encompasses the singular law of Eden—God is God and we are not."[10]

The taking of this fruit, beautiful to look at and good to the taste, was a rejection of God Himself. It was an invitation to death. James writes of the pervasive and deadly fruit of sin, declaring, "after desire has conceived, it gives birth to sin, and when sin is fully grown, it gives birth to death" (James 1:15). Sin is often depicted in pop culture as kind of harmless and edgy. We have TV shows provocatively named *Malice* or *Greed* and even ice-cream bars are declared sinfully delightful, but sin is the poison that has infected God's good world. Michael Bird writes, "What reigns on earth are not grace and blessings but death and decay. Death becomes an intrusive and tyrannical force in God's creation."[11]

An intrusive and tyrannical force, ruining human lives. Look around you. Read the headlines. You know. The world is not as it should be. Kids gunned down in our schools and cities. Corruption in the highest offices. Humans striving for power and money and sexual gratification, leaving the weak in their wake.

"Take and eat" seems so inviting, such a harmless indulgence, such a fleeting moment. And yet we can imagine that Eve would regret this moment for the rest of her life. "So simple the act, so hard its undoing. God will taste poverty and death before 'take and eat' become verbs of salvation,"[12] writes Derek Kidner.

✦ Saved by Childbirth ✦

So how did "take and eat" become, to quote Kidner, "verbs of salvation"? We find this in perhaps one of the most controversial verses in the New Testament, Paul's declaration in 1 Timothy 2:13–14:

For Adam was formed first, then Eve. And Adam was not deceived, but the woman was deceived and transgressed. But she will be saved through childbearing, if they continue in faith, love, and holiness, with good sense.

Saved by childbearing. This passage is embedded in instructions for leadership roles in the church, but it is often misunderstood. Paul is not here saying that women are by nature more gullible or easily deceived, but that the lies of the serpent went directly at God's design for His world. In tempting Eve, he circumvented Adam and circumvented God, preying on the vulnerability of Eve.

God's creation order is not about inferiority, as so many who read Genesis and 1 Timothy claim, but about stewardship and servant-hood. Though Christians disagree on the exact implications, it cannot be denied that God intentionally built into His creation genuine and complementary differences between men and women, differences many seek to blur while others seek to exploit, trampling on God's good design for our flourishing.

But more importantly, Paul is pointing to something beautiful in creation and in the gospel hope that is delivered in the midst of the curse of Genesis 3: women are central to the storyline of Scripture. Though birth is now accompanied by pain since the fall, the privilege of giving birth is God's sign of His love for humanity. Every single difficulty in childbirth is a reminder of the fateful day when Eve, speaking for all of us, yielded to the seduction of the serpent, and yet every single birth is a sign of God's promise to crush the head of that serpent. This is why the angel said to a young and vulnerable Jewish girl named Mary, "Blessed are you among women" (Luke 1:42). Mary stands at the apex of God's covenant with humanity. Jesus, the fulfillment of

Genesis 3:15, the seed of the woman, the greatest of Eve's grandsons, come to rescue a world corrupted by her deception.

We must see God's design for men and women, not as a cruel attempt to push down women but to elevate them as coequal image-bearers who work side by side with their brothers for their flourishing and God's glory. This is what Paul is getting at in 1 Timothy 2. This is the vision of God's kingdom community.

Amy Gannett writes, "As those who believe God has designed men and women equally in his image and made us equally vital to his kingdom work, we believe God loves women, and his design . . . for the home and . . . the church expresses his love."[13] The way God has ordered creation, the way He orders the family and the way He gathers redeemed men and women in His new covenant community is not about power or striving, but about sacrifice.

Ever since Eden, men and women have jostled and strived for supremacy and power. But God intends to restore what Satan has so thoroughly corrupted. Marriage then both looks backward and it points forward. The biblical vision of men and women in exclusive sexual union has its roots in creation. Jesus and Paul both quote Genesis's call for men and women to leave their parents and cleave to one another in self-giving love reserved only for this institution that images Christ and His church.

And yet marriage is a temporary signpost to something greater, the eternal union of Christ and His church. Adam sacrificed his body for his bride, and so it is that the second Adam sacrificed for His bride. From Adam's side came Eve, and from Jesus' side came the blood that redeems the church. It's not just Eve who is "saved by childbirth," but every single Christian who finds grace through being born again in

Christ. "Motherhood teaches women the imagery and language of the gospel on an intensely personal level," writes Jen Wilkin. "How appropriate the intertwined imagery of childbirth and the Cross: the necessary spilling of blood for the commencement of life, great loss holding hands with great gain."[14]

Eve would see heartbreak unfold in her own family. She'd see her son killed by another son. She would see God's beautiful world descend into depravity. The Bible tells us that Adam lived to be over 900 years old. We can presume, but don't know, that Eve likely lived most of those years. And yet Eve is a faint shadow of Mary, another woman with a special calling, who would see her own Son unjustly killed, whose sacrifice would be accepted by God. Jesus would reverse Eve's regret and our regret. Eve lived between two worlds—the world of Eden that she left and a new world, marred by sin, her sin, our sin.

We live in this in-between, the world we long for and the world we inhabit. The marriage you dream of and the marriage you experience. The career you wish you had and the career you have. We live with shattered dreams of Eden. But there is a third place beyond the Eden we've lost and the brokenness in which we live. God is taking us somewhere, to a new city, Eden fulfilled.

Adam and Eve began in the garden, naked and unashamed. Their quest to usurp God, to be all-knowing, thrust the humans into a cycle of shame and regret. But the second Adam went to the cross naked and ashamed so we could be clothed in the pure white robes of righteousness of Christ. We will never go back to the naked innocence of Eden, but we will go forward toward that new city clothed in perfect white clothes, made clean. Just as God slew the innocent animals to cover their shame, so God provided a perfect lamb slain to cover our shame.

◆ A Lonely Jesus for a Lonely People ◆

I want to revisit those words of Genesis 2:18. It is not good for humans to be alone. Moses understood this in Genesis. But do you know who really understood how bad it is to be alone? Jesus.

Adam experienced the temporary ache of loneliness, so much so that when he saw Eve he exclaimed, "At last!" But the second Adam was once truly alone. Stretched out on a cruel instrument of Roman torture, the One who didn't sin bore the curse in full for Adam's sin, for your sin, for mine. So much so that He cried out, "My God, my God, why have you abandoned me?"

Jesus came to erase the loneliness image-bearers have because of sin, that vile poison that entered Eden. The serpent-crusher chose loneliness that day on Golgotha, so we would never again have to be alone.

> Adam experienced the temporary ache of loneliness — but the second Adam was once truly alone.

Humans need community with our most important relationships, but ultimately, we need, we crave, we long for, community with the One who once walked with His people in the cool of the garden, the triune God who created us in His image and breathed into us the breath of life. No amount of human community, however rich, can replace the longing we have for God. For everyone who has ever felt alone, the promise whispered to Eve is the promise whispered to you: you can both known and be known by the One who formed you.

CHAPTER THREE

The Deceiver

Satan, Fallen from Glory, Father of Lies

You can't play with a serpent like the Devil
and not expect to get a snakebite.[1]

—TONY EVANS

I was standing on a street corner in Raleigh, about ready to get into an Uber to go to the airport and fly home to Nashville, when I got a text from my daughter Emma.

"There is a snake in the garage and Mom is hitting it with the hedge trimmer." And then a few minutes later I received an image of a decapitated garden snake, the results of my wife's assault on this insidious reptile.

Angela's adventure with the snake was not, as Bible students know, the first encounter between a woman and a snake. The idyllic setting of Eden was disrupted by the seductive charms of a slithering serpent.

Today we have a lot of images of what the tempter might look like, mostly false ideas from pop culture. We imagine a hideous-looking creature who announces his danger before he arrives. But this is not the case with this garden snake. The Bible says that he was among the most beautiful of God's creatures and more cunning than "any other beast of the field" (Gen. 3:1 ESV). This word *arum* is a kind of neutral adjective. At times, shrewdness is presented as a trait worth pursuing (Prov. 1:4; 8:5), and at times it is seen as a negative trait (Job 5:12; 15:5).[2] It's also worth noticing that the serpent was a "beast of the field." The snake was part of the animal kingdom, inhabited, of course, by Satan. His identity is unmasked later in Revelation 12:9. But Satan appropriated the most beautiful of God's creation, perverting this for wicked ends.

So when the serpent slithered up to Eve, she wasn't threatened at first. He didn't approach with horns and tongues of fire, with pitchforks and a red suit. Instead, her temptation came on the back of something beautiful. "The snake does not appear as the devil to the woman. The voice of temptation does not come as the voice of evil. If Satan is present in the story of Genesis 3, he is wearing a careful mask. He is hidden the ordinariness and the everydayness of a creature in the Garden,"[3] David Atkinson writes.

Don't miss this way of deceit from the enemy of our souls. He doesn't often come through the front door, announcing his malevolent intentions. Instead, he sneaks in the back door, charming and attractive. Eve wasn't scandalized by the sight of the serpent. He wasn't hideous and grotesque. Instead, he was the object of her fascination.

And yet his power, then and now, is overstated. The serpent was a mere animal, a created being. He may have dazzled and strung together spellbinding words, perhaps in and of itself a sign that there was something special, an animal that can speak with humans. Yet this serpent was still a member of the animal kingdom, over which God had given Adam and Eve dominion. We wonder how long the serpent lay in the weeds, waiting to strike. Perhaps this creature, as some have speculated, could have been like one of the seraphim mentioned in

Isaiah 14.[4] Part of the cosmic curse God pronounced on snakes is that they would forever slither on their bellies. So could this serpent have had four legs, perhaps some wings? Could it have been the wonder of the garden, beautiful, a source of daily entertainment and inspiration?

Such subtle temptations have been a regular feature of the devil since that fateful day in Eden. He is cunning and presents himself in flattering ways (even as an angel of light—see 2 Cor. 11:14). As he roams about seeking whom he may devour (1 Peter 5:8), his search is very subtle.

✦ Who Is Satan and How Did He ✦
Get into the Garden?

So who is Satan and how did he arrive in God's beautiful garden? First, a little backstory on the devil. He is not actually identified first as Satan here in Genesis 1, but the rest of Scripture makes it clear that this was no ordinary snake. Revelation 12:9, for instance, connects Satan with the snake: "the ancient serpent, who is called the devil and Satan, the one who deceives the whole world." He is first called Satan in the book of Job, a book many believe was the first Old Testament book written. Job pulls back the curtain on a conversation between God and Satan, revealing both the supernatural power of Satan and his limits under God's rule. Satan is allowed by God to reach out his hand and afflict Job with suffering, such as the loss of his wealth, his children, and his health. And yet he can't take Job's life and he has no power over Job's soul.

Sometimes we assume that the cosmic battle between God and Satan, predicted by God in Genesis 3:15, is a fight among equals. But

God is superior to Satan, who is a mere created being. John's gospel tells us that through Christ "all things exist" and Colossians 1:16–17 makes clear that everything in the universe was created by Him:

> *For everything was created by him,*
> *in heaven and on earth,*
> *the visible and the invisible,*
> *whether thrones or dominions*
> *or rulers or authorities—*
> *all things have been created through him and for him.*
> *He is before all things,*
> *and by him all things hold together.*

Sometimes we assume that the battle between God and Satan is a fight among equals.

Even thrones or dominions are created by and subject to the Lord's rule. We don't know exactly when, but somewhere in God's creative process, before He rested on the seventh day, He created angelic beings (Job 38:4, 7). The Bible describes the devil as a fallen angel, who tried to rise up and become like God. In Luke 10, Jesus says, "I watched Satan fall from heaven like lightning." Revelation describes a cosmic battle in Heaven:

> Then war broke out in heaven: Michael and his angels fought against the dragon. The dragon and his angels also fought, but he could not prevail, and there was no place for them in heaven any longer. So the great dragon was thrown out—the ancient serpent, who is called the devil and Satan, the one who deceives the whole world. He was thrown to earth, and his angels with him. (Rev. 12:7–9)

So sometime in the creation timeline, Satan and a cohort of angels rose up against God and were defeated and kicked out of heaven. Two passages in the Old Testament seem to describe Satan's fall this way. In Isaiah 14, the prophet is declaring a word about the wicked king of Babylon, but the language seems to go beyond the status of that earthly king and describe Satan's attempt to usurp God and take control of the cosmos:

> *Shining morning star,*
> *how you have fallen from the heavens!*
> *You destroyer of nations,*
> *you have been cut down to the ground.*
> *You said to yourself,*
> *"I will ascend to the heavens;*
> *I will set up my throne*
> *above the stars of God.*
> *I will sit on the mount of the gods' assembly,*
> *in the remotest parts of the North.*
> *I will ascend above the highest clouds;*
> *I will make myself like the Most High."*
> *But you will be brought down to Sheol*
> *into the deepest regions of the Pit.* (Isa. 14:12–15)

The King James Version translates "morning star" to "Lucifer, Son of the Morning." Other translations render it "Daystar, Son of Dawn." It seems Jesus is referring to this passage, given that language similar to Isaiah's is used in Luke to describe Satan being cast out of heaven. Jesus wants to connect the dots and help us understand Satan's fall.[5]

Notice how often "I will" is used here. *I will ascend to the heavens. I will set up my throne above the stars of God. I will sit on the mount of the gods' assembly. I will make myself like the Most High.* This is Satan's declaration that his status as an angel wasn't enough for him. He demanded to climb to God's level, to be worshiped like God. To make himself *like the Most High* is language that alludes to God (Gen. 14:18, 19). It is an attempt to knock *El Elyon* off His throne and be worshiped. Says James Montgomery Boice, "This is what Lucifer wanted to be. His rebellion was not a request for God to move over so that he might share God's throne. It was a thrust at God himself. It was an attempt to put God out so that Satan might take his place as possessor of the heavens and the earth."[6]

When Satan appeals to Eve by saying to her that by disobeying God she would be like God, you can hear echoes of Satan's grasping for power in heaven. This is part of Satan's program, the one whom Jesus called "a liar and the father of lies" (John 8:44).

One more passage in Scripture seems to describe Satan's fall. In these verses in Ezekiel, the prophet is describing the king of Tyre—but there are deeper allusions here, it seems, to a supernatural being:

> *Thus says the Lord God:*
>
> *"You were the signet of perfection,*
> *full of wisdom and perfect in beauty.*
> *You were in Eden, the garden of God;*
> *every precious stone was your covering,*
> *sardius, topaz, and diamond,*
> *beryl, onyx, and jasper,*
> *sapphire, emerald, and carbuncle;*

> *and crafted in gold were your settings*
> *and your engravings.*
> *On the day that you were created*
> *they were prepared.*
> *You were an anointed guardian cherub.*
> *I placed you; you were on the holy mountain of God;*
> *in the midst of the stones of fire you walked.*
> *You were blameless in your ways*
> *from the day you were created,*
> *till unrighteousness was found in you."* (Ezek. 28:12–15 ESV)

If this is referring to Satan before his fall, and I think it is, the passage describes in detail his beauty and wisdom. It appears he was perhaps the top angel in God's heavenly realm. This passage also alludes to Eden, which would correspond to the serpent's ability to both know God's instructions to Adam and Eve and have a unique vantage point to initiate the temptation to disobey.

Biblical scholars throughout the ages have disagreed on these passages and whether they refer to Satan. But we can be sure from Scripture that Satan, once a beautiful angel, was cast out of heaven, an epic battle witnessed by Jesus (Luke 10). It appears that once cast from heaven, Satan determined to deceive God's image-bearers. Having failed to usurp the Almighty, he whispered lies to God's prized creation, inhabiting the skin of a serpent. His words ring with bitterness and jealousy: "God knows . . . you will be like God." The one who wanted to usurp God, urging humans to repeat his grasp for power.

In disobeying God, Adam and Eve handed over power to Satan and his fallen horde of demons. Paul describes him in Ephesians as the "ruler of the power of the air" (Eph. 2:2) and the "god of this age" (2 Cor. 4:4). Jesus referred to him as "the ruler of this world" (John 12:31). He has power to destroy and deceive, to inflict suffering (as in the life of Job). He prowls the earth seeking to devour (1 Peter 5:8) humans, designing schemes to snare and trap men and women in evil (2 Cor. 2:11). Jesus said Satan was a "murderer from the beginning" (John 8:44).

✦ Did God *Really* Say? ✦

Oh, but this "murderer from the beginning" didn't march into Eden looking like, well . . . a merchant of death. Moses writes that the serpent, this shrewdest of beasts, came to Eve as he comes to us, with a custom-designed plan to get between her and her God.

Old Testament scholar John Collins notices that while Genesis elsewhere refers to God as "The LORD God," connecting God to His covenant relationship as Yahweh, the serpent drops this, as if to take Eve's focus away from God's faithfulness to His promises, His personal relationship with His people. "By dropping the covenant name, the serpent is advancing his temptation by diverting the woman's attention from the relationship the Lord had established. The woman's use of it shows that she is trapped, and we begin to have a clue as to how she could be led into disobedience; by forgetting the covenant."[7]

The devil's approach was not just surgical, but also supernatural. Let's remember that God had given Adam and Eve dominion over the animal kingdom. There is no record anywhere else of animals talking. So here Satan perverts creation and gives the snake a speaking gift, surely wowing Eve, planting seeds of doubt in her mind that God, the One who created her, perhaps was not as uniquely powerful as she thought. And the singular question he leads off with is one that has been repeated since Eden, the root of every move away from God, big and small, *Has God really said?*

This is not a sincere question, a moment of doubt, an inquiry for the Almighty. God welcomes questions, as evidenced by their presence in Scripture, coming off the lips of some of His most beloved. David, Job, Jeremiah, Paul, and a host of others join people who, throughout the centuries, have lifted their finite minds to heaven in bewilderment. God can handle our questions.

And yet there is something diabolical about these words from the serpent. "Satan smoothly maneuvers Eve into what may appear as a sincere theological discussion, but he subverts obedience and distorts perspective by emphasizing God's prohibition, not his provision, reducing God's command to a question, doubting his sincerity, defaming his motives, and denying the truthfulness of his threat."[8]

This is not a question of wanting to know more about God, to go further in and further up into understanding His good purposes. Instead, this is willful mockery. *Can you believe God said this?* Or: *Did He really just say that? You don't believe that stuff, do you?*

The questions appealed to Eve's vanity. It put her in the question of evaluating God. The one formed from dust judging the hands that formed her, the clay clapping back at the potter, the created having a word of advice for the Creator. Not only is it blasphemous, it's rather ridiculous. Imagine a work of art rebuking the artist. Imagine a building shouting back at the architect. Imaging a sculpture with some ideas for the sculptor. Even these examples pale in comparison to this devilish appeal in Eden, because human creators can be flawed, can produce faulty designs, can fail in their endeavors, but this is the

One who breathed the world into existence and it was good.

Did God really say? is the road to rebellion. It's a question that is asked today, sometimes by God's own people. In a culture that increasingly sees Christianity as not just weird, but dangerous, the gospel and all its implications will be met by this kind of derision and Christians will be tempted to find loopholes to God's law.

And the serpent continues, not just mocking God's right to rule His own universe, but distorting God's instructions. "Did God really say you can't eat from any tree?" Satan knows what God said. But he twists it to make God look like a cosmic curmudgeon, holding out on His people, a tried-and-true tactic of the enemies of creation. God had given Adam and Eve freedom to enjoy the lush and bountiful provision of Eden, restricting one tree. This is a favorite tactic of the enemy. You can hear this today. *Does God really hate sex? Does God really hate money? Does God want you to be miserable?*

Or we work backward. *The God I know wouldn't care who I marry or what I do with my body or how I spend my money. God is love.* And like Eve, we are tempted to reckon, not with what God has said, but with what a distorted version of what He said. This is the same approach Satan would take centuries later, not in a garden, but in a desert, and the target was not the innocent Eve, but the perfect Jesus, who refused to be a party to the devil's attempt to undermine the Father. But unlike Jesus, Eve answered the serpent with her own half-truths. She responds by correctly pointing out that there was only one forbidden tree, but she too layers on subtle distortions by misquoting God's Word, "You must not eat it or touch it." God didn't say the fruit could not be touched, only that it could not be consumed.

You see, she was already playing the devil's game here, already having brought her, an image-bearer, down to the level of a beast, treating the serpent as an equal. Instead, her response should have been to "resist the devil" so the snake would flee (James 4:7).

The focus of the devil's campaign of mistrust is to get Eve to center her behavior, not around the covenant between her and her Creator, not in gratitude at the bountiful blessings at her disposal, but on her own desires and the one area where God asks her to resist and obey. These are small-scale seeds of mistrust he is sowing in her heart. "The serpent touches the woman at the one small, trivial point in her life where she was not ready to give everything over to God," David Atkinson writes. "The serpent touches us at that one thing in our lives where we would rather God did not trouble us."[9]

Here, we see echoes of the appeal to the rich young ruler who, though following God in every other area, was unwilling to yield in the one area where he refused to make Jesus Lord (Matt. 19:22). And we see ourselves, troubled by God in the one area where we desire to be our own god. Like the rich young ruler, like Eve, we too go away sad.

But the deception grows. This campaign of subterfuge bores in, the assault on the authority of God's Word finding its mark. *You shall not surely die* was Satan's response to Eve's recounting of God's pronouncement of judgment for disobedience. And in here we see the danger of half-truths. Did Eve drop dead when her teeth first sank into the fruit? Of course not. She and Adam lived on for hundreds of years and bore generations of children. She didn't physically die. But in a way she would, because what God was saying is that this death they would suffer was both spiritual and physical. They could no longer live in immortality.

Sin introduced death into the human experience. Physical death that brought disease and despair, violence and mayhem, genocide and war, into God's good world. And yet when sin conceives, it not only brings forth physical death (James 1:15), it brings in relational and spiritual death. It would divide men against women, brother against brother, would pit ethnic groups in perpetual struggle for survival. And ultimately, it would pit human beings against their Creator.

This is the pernicious lie of sin. The enemy promises only pleasure and no pain, but we know this just isn't true. Enslavement to our desires is like a walking death. Our world is full of people who outwardly exhibit the signs of joy and inwardly are empty, without hope. We see tragic death everywhere, stalking us and haunting us. Ephesians reminds us that, separated from God, we are the walking dead (Eph. 2:1).

This lie is whispered every day. *You'll get away with it. Nobody will know. Nothing will happen.* "It's the serpent's word against God's and the first doctrine to be denied is judgment."[10] We, like Eve, are so keen to hear this false word. We live in the wreckage of this lie. Around us is the shrapnel of our rejection of God's good way, we have the "aroma of death" on us (2 Cor. 2:16) and yet post-Eden, we have hope, for there is One whom the Bible says would "taste death for everyone" (Heb. 2:9). Satan was wrong. If you sin, when you sin, you will surely die, both spiritually and physically, and yet Jesus experienced death for us so we might look death in the face and declare with Paul, "You have no sting!" (see 1 Cor. 15:55–57).

The temptation of Eve and the temptation for every one of us is, in Satan's words, *You shall be like God, knowing good and evil.* The one who couldn't be like God offers his same losing proposition to image-bearers. *God knows you will be like Him.*

In a sense, Satan is right here. God's prohibition on the tree of knowledge of good and evil is a protection against a kind of all-knowing that humans were never created for. We were never made to bear the weight of omniscience. We were created to bear the image of God, but we make lousy gods. We are not built for deity. This is a great temptation of our age, an age of science and discovery and unlimited information at our fingertips. Data is rushing at us in torrents unseen in human history. If we are not careful, our desire to know, the hunger and curiosity about the world, can quickly turn into the age-old temptation in the garden, where Eve looked at the forbidden and wrongly concluded that it was "desirable for obtaining wisdom." Curiosity about God's world without trust in the God who made the world ends up in death.

> We were created to bear the image of God, but we make lousy gods.

This perverse quest for knowing is, as Bruce Waltke explains, not a hunger for more information but a "hunger for power that comes from knowledge that has the potential for evil ends as well as for good . . . Knowledge of good and evil is not a neutral state, desired maturity, or an advancement of humanity . . . God desires to save humans from their inclination for ethical autonomy."[11]

This is why God's judgment on Adam and Eve is actually an act of grace. To that lying messenger of death, Satan, God declares, "I will put hostility between you and the woman." God severs the alliance and though Satan prowls and tempts and destroys, he will not have the last word over humans. And the expulsion from the garden, though painful, is another sign of grace, for now that they possess this evil kind of knowing, this sinful hearts, they must not approach the tree of life. Waltke continues, "Because Adam and Eve have attained this sinful state, they must not eat of the tree of life and are consigned forever to the forbidden state of being inclined to choose their own code of ethics."[12] Even in this curse, God is rescuing humans from a state of perpetual death.

✦ The One Who Faced Temptation ✦

The serpent's appeals, so crafty and surgical, are repeated by the enemy every day since that fateful day in the garden. Like Eve, we hear the murmurs, the lies, the subtle voice of the enemy. And the myth, this side of Eden, is that to sin, to yield to the voice of Satan, to indulge our desires, is the essence of being human.

And yet we must not only see ourselves as Genesis 3 people, fallen, but as Genesis 1 people as well. In attempting to be like God, to sin, is to be less than human. Eve should have resisted the serpent. But in her indulgence she didn't become like God, but she became like an animal. There is a reason that evil is depicted in the book of Revelation as a dragon. Temptation preys on animal instincts. It tells us we are nothing more than our desires. Russell Moore reminds us of what happens when we sin:

> You start to see yourself as either special or as hopeless, and thus the normal boundaries don't seem to apply. It might be that you are involved in certain patterns right now and that you would, if asked, be able to tell me exactly why they are morally and ethically wrong. It's not that you are deficient in the cognitive ability to diagnose the situation. It's instead that you slowly grow to believe that your situation is exceptional ("I am a god"), and then you find all kinds of reasons why this technically isn't theft or envy or hatred or fornication or abuse

of power or whatever ("I am able to discern good and evil"). Or you believe you are powerless before what you want ("I am an animal") and can therefore escape accountability ("I will not surely die"). You've forgotten who you are. You are a creature. You are also a king or a queen. You are not a beast, and you are not a god. That issue is where temptation begins.[13]

But what can we do in the face of temptation? How can we resist the advances of the enemy? Corrupted by the fall, we can't help but sin. And there is a way in which religion has us back in the garden fixing the mess we made with our own effort, but we know that on our best days we say yes to sin. "Not today, Satan" is a myth.

Except there is one, Jesus, that seed of the women, who took on human flesh and was "tempted in every way . . . yet without sin" (Heb. 4:15). He walked through a desert of temptation, assaulted with the same lies as Eve and yet emerged sinless, the perfect God-man. But what Jesus has for us is not just a good example of how to resist the devil, but one who not only said no to Satan, but went to the cross and in His agony, cried "It is finished," defeating the enemy powers. Paul writes in Colossians 2:15 that Jesus "disarmed the rulers and authorities and disgraced them publicly; he triumphed over them in him."

> **"Not today, Satan" is a myth.**

So while we can't go back to Eden, we also don't walk through the desert of temptation alone. Jesus went before us, resisted Satan's overtures, and went to the cross, then rose again, defeating sin, death, and the grave. Satan still roams the earth seeking to devour, Satan is temporarily the prince and power of the air and the ruler of this world, but he is on a leash. And while we shouldn't underestimate him, we should also not live in fear. Those who are in Christ can take comfort in the words the aging apostle John wrote to a church beleaguered by persecution and despair: "The one who is in you is greater than the one who is in the world" (1 John 4:4).

And ultimately the Bible tells us that Satan's end is hell. He will be banished there forever, when Jesus returns, to tempt the nations no more (Rev. 20:3). Satan, Michael Heiser reminds us, "remains active in the world until the final judgment, blinding the minds of people to prevent them from joining the kingdom of Jesus, but he has no accusation to bring against those who belong to Christ. His rightful claim over their lives in the realm of the dead is nullified through the resurrection of Christ and the union with Christ for all who believe the gospel. In the final judgment, Satan's domicile, the realm of the dead, is transformed into the place of his torment."[14]

Until then, we can rest in spiritual power, refusing to fight the devil on his terms and in our own strength. The Bible promises us that the Spirit of God empowers us to overcome temptation:

> *No temptation has come upon you except what is common to humanity. But God is faithful; he will not allow you to be tempted beyond what you are able, but with the temptation he will also provide the way out so that you may be able to bear it. (1 Cor. 10:13)*

That way of escape is not our own self-sufficiency, our own attempt to help ourselves, but the resources we have as citizens of God's new kingdom. We draw on spiritual power, available for us. "For although we live in the flesh, we do not wage war according to the flesh, since the weapons of our warfare are not of the flesh, but are powerful through God for the demolition of strongholds" (2 Cor. 10:4).

We fight sin; we resist temptation; we throw back the lies of the enemy with God's full armor (Eph. 6). We will not win every battle. We will make Eve's choice every day and multiple times a day, but on this side of Calvary, we don't have to sit in our sin, but can draw upon God's rich provision of mercy and find forgiveness and freedom (1 John 1:9). And the devil, whose name means "accuser," cannot make a claim on our soul, cannot pin guilt on us, because Christ has taken our guilt and shame (Rev. 12:10).

Satan is powerful. He's a lion who roars. And yet we should not ascribe God-like characteristics to him. He's not all-powerful, not all-knowing. He cannot read our thoughts and does not know the future. He captains a horde of demons, but they are on the losing side. And in the power of the Spirit of God, the devil can be resisted. The serpent has unleashed evil in God's good creation, but we can say, with the reformer Martin Luther, about our foe:

> The Prince of darkness grim,—
> We tremble not for him;
> His rage we can endure,
> For lo! his doom is sure,—
>   One little word shall fell him![15]

The Slain Sacrifice

Abel and the Cost of Discipleship

*Abel's blood spoke from the earth and cried for justice (Gen. 4:10),
while Christ's blood speaks from heaven and announces mercy for
sinners. Abel's blood made Cain feel guilty (and rightly so) and
drove him away in despair (Gen. 4:13–15), but Christ's blood
frees us from guilt and has opened the way into the presence of
God. Were it not for the blood of the new covenant, we could not
enter this heavenly city.*[1]

—Warren Wiersbe

In December of 2020, the stillness of Christmas morning in Pemi,
a small village in northeastern Nigeria, was shattered by the sounds
of gunshots as Boko Haram militants attacked Christians at worship,
invading homes, burning down a church, slaughtering men, women,
and children, and killing the local priest.[2]

In March of 2011, a young girl named Rocio Pino opened the
door of her home in Colombia, a door she had opened previously
to share the good news of Jesus with a guerilla fighter, who accepted
her gift of a Bible. This time, Rocio was greeted by the terrorist group
FARC, who shot her to death.[3]

Sergei Bessarab was a notorious member of the Tajikistan underworld, spending eighteen years in prison for violent crimes. But during one of these prison stays, a fellow prisoner shared about Jesus with him, a friend who himself had learned about Jesus through the prison ministry of the Baptist churches in Tajikistan. Sergei became a Christian and turned his passion for crime into a passion for Jesus, leading the prison chapel ministry. When he got out of prison, he started a church in his hometown, one that began growing as they heard the testimony of this former mobster turned pastor. The local newspaper began to cover this movement of God, which alarmed Sergei's former friends, who were threatened by his new faith. One day, while Sergei was leading worship in his home church, bullets shot through the front window, eventually killing Sergei in front of his wife.[4]

Sergei, Rocio, the slain priest in Nigeria, and thousands of others whose faces and names we don't know, whose spilt blood rarely graces the headlines that scroll across our timelines, are part of a long line of faithful followers of God who were willing to obey and declare their faith despite persecution. These courageous brothers and sisters are heirs of the world's very first martyr (Matt. 23:35), a man with a life so obscure none of his words are recorded, a man whose very name means "vapor" or "breath."[5]

✦ He Is Abel ✦

Kicked out of the garden, Adam and Eve nevertheless clung to God's promise that human life would continue. Their nakedness now covered by skins from animal sacrifices initiated by God, they, like us, would live in a world of contradictions. Creation, still beautiful and majestic and ready to be subdued, would now fight back with thorns and this-tles. Human relationships, once free of the petty sins that divide, were now beset by civilizational struggles for power and supremacy. And the place where once Eve and Adam had walked with God in the cool of the day was now forbidden to them, sinners unable to venture into the presence of a holy God.

And yet Adam and Eve would not resist God's judgment but would submit themselves to it, coming together to begin God's work to be fruitful, to multiply their seed, and to fill the earth. Satan's work would continue in just the second generation, but so would the work of God to establish a seed of the faithful from whom a Messiah would come.

Genesis doesn't tell us about all of Adam and Eve's children—we know they must have had quite a few in the hundreds of years in which they lived—but it does tell us about two who are important for us to understand what God is doing in the world.

In this chapter, I'd like to explore the second-born child, or at least the second child mentioned in Genesis. We can't be certain that Cain and Abel were the very first children born to the first couple, though the text kind of implies this. Scripture often doesn't give us a chronology of events, so it can be easy for modern readers to speed up the timeline. In any case, imagine what it must have been like for Adam and Eve to look on in wonder at the birth of their two sons. I remember what it was like to stand in the delivery room and hold in my hands each of our four children as they came into the world. There is hardly a greater feeling than beholding your own offspring and feel-ing the joy of God's promise of life continue into another generation.

Imagine, then, the joy Eve must have felt in witnessing, for the first time in history, the miracle of human birth. God's promises that

Eve would be the mother of all living were coming to pass in front of them. Imagine Adam's joy at seeing his two sons. Though they'd experience the heartbreak of seeing their sinful choices passed down to their progeny, it couldn't erase the euphoria of witnessing the wonder of human life.

Imagine the joy Eve must have felt in witnessing, for the first time in history, the miracle of human birth.

When their second child arrived, he was given a name, Abel or *hubel*. This is a Hebrew word that means "breath" or "brevity of life." Moses doesn't really tell us why Eve gave her second-born child this name. She could not have understood, as she wrapped her little boy in her arms, as she fed him and changed him and hugged his little body, as she watched him grow up, that Abel's life would be but a vapor, snatched too early by an eruption of violence, a demonstration that sin, when conceived, brings forth death (James 1:15).

I wonder if she named her second son "breath" because she also knew the story of her own life and the life of her beloved. It was the breath of God that gave Adam and Eve life, and it was from the bone that protects the function of breath, the rib, from which she was formed and crafted by the hands of God. This same idea of breath and wind would come to symbolize, in God's Word, the work of God through His Spirit in creating (Gen. 1) and re-creating (Acts 1; John 20:22). "By his breath," Job writes, "the heavens gained their beauty; his hand pierced the fleeing serpent" (Job 26:13).

Genesis tells us little about Abel's childhood. Imagine growing up in the still-raw creation, exploring the animal kingdom. It is likely that Abel had quite a few siblings, perhaps hundreds, given how long

Adam lived (over 900 years!). Imagine him running up and down the hillsides with his brothers and sisters, through the wooded forests and across the fertile plains. Scripture tells us Abel was a shepherd, but we can wonder how he learned to care for sheep. Did he watch his father Adam? Did he have natural instincts, learned by watching the flocks and figuring how to lead and guide them? God made animal skins for Adam and Eve after the fall (Gen. 3:21). Perhaps they were made of sheep and this began, perhaps, the practice of raising them for clothing and food. We do know that shepherding is a theme for leadership in Scripture. Abel was the first of many shepherds: David, Amos, the shepherds who heard the good word of Jesus' birth, and of course Jesus Himself, the self-proclaimed Good Shepherd.

✦ **Of Whom the World Was Not Worthy** ✦

It is ultimately Abel's shepherding that brings us to the climax of his conflict with his brother, Cain. Genesis tells us there is a moment where both brothers bring a sacrifice to offer to God. It is unlikely that this is the first time both brothers participated in this rite. It's likely they learned this from Adam and Eve, who first saw God slay animals as a way of covering their shame and as a symbol of the unfolding salvation history, a vivid illustration that the shedding of innocent blood would be required to cover sin. It's possible these early rituals were a foreshadowing of what would come later, with the people of God and the system of sacrifice to God.

Genesis tells us that Abel brought the best of his livestock, the firstborn. Abel brought his best as a sacrifice to the Lord. Remember, the relationship between humans and their Creator was no longer intimate, but separated by sin. So approaching God would now require a me-diating sacrifice. There isn't much detail in the text of Scripture about how often this would happen, where it would happen, how they ex-actly communicated with God. We are told, however, that God was pleased with Abel's offering:

> *And Abel also brought an offering—fat portions from some of the firstborn of his flock. The LORD looked with favor on Abel and his offering, but on Cain and his offering he did not look with favor. So Cain was very angry, and his face was downcast. (Gen. 4:4–5 NIV)*

Why did God accept Abel's offering and reject Cain's? It's hard to know. Some have speculated that because Abel brought a blood sacri-fice, it was accepted by God. After all, this is the pattern of atonement in the story of salvation. But we can't be completely sure about this, because there are other places where a grain offering is acceptable (Lev. 2:3). Perhaps we can find some clues in the way Moses describes Abel's offering: he brought the firstborn and the fatted portions, often con-sidered the most desirable parts of the animal.[6] Abel brought his best. But it seems that the most important reason God accepted Abel was not necessarily because of the type of sacrifice he brought, but because of his faith. Listen to the writer of Hebrews:

> *By faith Abel offered to God a better sacrifice than Cain did. By faith he was approved as a righteous man, because God approved his gifts, and even though he is dead, he still speaks through his faith. (Heb. 11:4)*

By faith, he offered a better sacrifice. *By faith,* he was approved as a righteous man. Kenneth Matthews says that God's response toward Cain and Abel "was not due to the nature of the gift per se, whether it was grain or animal, but the integrity of the giver. The narrative ties together the worshiper and his offering as God considers the merit of their individual worship . . . Unlike a human observer, God sees the condition of the human heart and weighs the motive of the worshiper (e.g., 1 Sam 16:7)."[7]

Martin Luther had a similar observation: "The fault lay not in the materials which were offered but in the person of him who brought the offering. The faith of the individual was the weight which added value to Abel's offering . . . Abel acknowledges that he is an untrustworthy and poor sinner. Therefore he takes refuge in God's mercy and believes that God is gracious and willing to show compassion."[8] Luther also speculates that this scene was similar to the scene centuries later, when another courageous prophet of God, Elijah, confronted false worship with a display on Mt. Carmel (1 Kings 18).

We don't really know if such a scene happened, but the writer of Hebrews makes it clear that Abel's sacrifice was an act of faith and obedience in God. And Jesus pointing to Abel as the first in a long and continuing line of martyrs helps us understand that Abel's sacrifice was not a mere religious ritual, but a deliberate and costly act of obedience. Could it be that Abel's humble faith, his acknowledgment of his own sin, his dependence on the Lord for forgiveness, made him a target for Cain's growing hostility?

How often did Cain taunt Abel, mock him for his devotion and obedience, dare him to approach the altar as cavalierly as Cain did? How tempted was Abel to yield to the pressure and approach God on his own terms instead of God's terms?

This was costly obedience. Too often we who live in relative comfort in the West fail to comprehend what it is to live for Jesus in a way that won't reward us with material possessions and worldly affirmation.

Abel went to the altar that day knowing it could cost him—and ultimately it did. His life was cut short. His brother would go on to build a family, and nations would arise out of his offspring. Not so Abel. On paper, his life seems a bit of a waste. Why not cut a few corners, why not avoid the risk, why not save his life?

But Jesus, who saw Abel's life and hailed him as the first martyr, says genuine faith is willing to follow Jesus in costly sacrifice: "For whoever wants to save his life will lose it, but whoever loses his life because of me will find it" (Matt. 16:25). The book of Hebrews says his life "still speaks" (Heb. 11:4). And so it does. His life was a vapor . . . his faith speaks volumes.

This is the true way of Jesus, but not a popular approach. We would rather be liked and loved, and are willing to sand off the rough edges of the gospel's implications to get that affirmation. We'd rather hear that God's desire for us is to reap endless and upwardly mobile riches and prosperity. But Abel did everything right, and he lost his life. Cain did everything wrong, and he saved it.

To be clear, we shouldn't seek martyrdom and sometimes we mistake our own inability to love and our desire to fight as "persecution." Sometimes we think we are brave because we say stupid and controversial things online. We look in the mirror and see a hero.

This was not Abel. His sacrifice was costly. His approach was humility and self-sacrifice. And it cost him his life. Martyrdom isn't self-martyrdom, declaring ourselves the brave ones on social media. It's the humble willingness to obey in the face of opposition.

But Jesus did say that if He were persecuted, so would we be (John 15:20). Jesus' brother James tells us that to be a "friend of the world" is to be in "hostility" toward the world. Every Christian faces this choice, be it those who suffer under the thumb of un-just governments overseas or those of us who face increasing backlash for what we believe. Abel understood the economy of heaven; that short-term suffering, a life as a vapor, is worth the greater reward of that life to come.

The writer of Hebrews, who began chapter 11 with Abel, ends this tour of the Bible's heroes, men and women who lived by faith, with this tribute to martyrs:

> *Destitute, afflicted, and mistreated. . . . The world was not worthy of them. . . . All these were approved through their faith, but they did not receive what was promised, since God had provided something better for us, so that they would not be made perfect without us. (Heb. 11:37–40)*

The world was not worthy of them. Then and now and in every generation since, following Christ despite the cost seems a waste, throwing a life away for something unseen. But Abel possessed something richer than the world's cheap gain, he had *faith.* Faith, this writer of Hebrews tells us, is "the substance of things hoped for, the evidence of things not seen" (Heb. 11:1 KJV).

Abel clung to the tiny sliver of hope embedded in the promise given to his parents, that out of the wreckage of sin, from the offspring of his family, would come a redeemer whose atoning sacrifice would cover his sin. Today, on this side of Calvary, we know more than Abel did about this son of Eve, this second Adam, who would make the world right.

Sometimes we think we are brave because we say stupid and controversial things online.

✦ Cries from the Ground ✦

Abel's life also points us to another important truth. It reveals God's heart for justice. When Abel followed his brother to the field that day, he probably didn't know it would be his last day on earth. But perhaps he sensed the growing hostility between him and his brother, perhaps he could feel the seething rage inside of Cain, maybe he knew he was headed into danger. We can speculate on how this went down—if Cain overpowered Abel with force, if he was the physically stronger brother, or if he ambushed him when he wasn't looking. It was a gross injustice, the shedding of the innocent blood of an image-bearer, a direct assault on God Himself. And yet what happened in that field that day wasn't done in secret, for the God who sees and hears, saw. God sees injustice and doesn't wink at it.

Moses writes that God declared that Abel's blood "cried to him" from the ground. And so it is with every drop of innocent blood spilled across time and eternity. God sees the aborted baby discarded in abortion mills. God sees the victims of violence on our city streets, the victims who quickly pass from the headlines. God sees the refugees and victims of trafficking. God sees when women are assaulted in their homes, when young children are abused, when political prisoners in places like North Korea are forced to live an existence barely above death in labor camps. Oh, He sees. God knows and as the judge of the earth will "do what is just" (Gen. 18:25).

And: "I have surely seen the affliction of my people who are in Egypt and have heard their cry because of their taskmasters. I know their sufferings" (Ex. 3:7 ESV), God would say centuries later, about His people stuck in bondage to a cruel king. Their blood cried to Him from the sands of Egypt.

Abel's blood, and the blood of every victim of injustice, cries out to the God of the universe. And yet Abel's blood also points us to the blood of another son of Eve whose blood was unjustly spilled:

God sees injustice and doesn't wink at it.

> *Jesus, the mediator of a new covenant, and to the sprinkled blood,*
> *which says better things than the blood of Abel. (Heb. 12:24)*

Abel's sacrifice was satisfactory to God as a sign of his faith, but Jesus' sacrifice is better. Abel's blood cries out for justice. Jesus' blood speaks mercy and grace for those who believe. Says scholar George Guthrie: "Abel's blood bore witness against Cain, indicating his guilt. Christ's blood, on the other hand, has won our forgiveness, 'crying out' that people of the new covenant are no longer guilty, having been cleansed completely from sin."[9]

In Jesus' death, we see both just punishment, exacted by God for sin, the sins of Adam, the sins of Cain, and our own sins; and we see forgiveness and reconciliation between God and sinners. This is the better word spoken by Jesus, the one that those who believe can hear, a word that says to us, "It is finished."

CHAPTER FIVE

The Marked

Cain and the Price of Self-Worship

*The "way of Cain" is the way of religion without faith,
righteousness based on character and good works. The "way
of Cain" is the way of pride, a man establishing his own
righteousness and rejecting the righteousness of God that
comes through faith in Christ.*[1]

—WARREN WIERSBE

There is nothing as intoxicating as holding your own child for the
very first time. Sixteen years later as I watch my daughter drive off
and go to work at her summer job, I remember those first few moments
at Northwest Community Hospital, the very last day of the year in
2004. There is a weird thing that happens with dads. For dads, we are
excited when we get the news that our wives are pregnant. There is a
low-level nervousness about how this whole parenting thing is going to
work out. But even though we feel the baby kicking and see the grainy
images on the sonogram and we paint the nursery light blue, we don't
really *feel* like a dad, do we? Well, until that little child, freshly scrubbed
of the blood and assorted fluids of childbirth, is nestled in our arms, that
standard but precious hospital blanket wrapping her up like a burrito.

So many emotions arise when your child is born. I remember thinking about the ways I wanted to parent, about what my kid could potentially be. You feel that your kids are blank slates upon which you can write your preferred destiny for them. Not so. You see, God, in His inscrutable and sometimes maddening mystery, has created pathways for our kids that we could not map out for them even if we wanted to.

Those mixed feelings of emotion and mystery, the seeming sense of unlimited potential we see when we first lay eyes on our progeny are multiplied infinitely in the experience of Eve. She saw her first-born open his eyes, let out one of those soft baby breaths or loud baby cries, and enter the world.

You can almost hear it in her voice. Moses records Eve's words, words every mother who has endured nine long months while a life grows inside, who has experienced the agony of labor. Sometimes I like the plainspoken clarity of the King James I grew up memorizing. *I have gotten a man from the LORD.* Perhaps the NIV is more accurate to the symbiotic partnership between God and a mother: *With the help of the LORD I have brought forth a man.* Every mother needs the Lord's help to bring forth a child.

> Perhaps she saw in her firstborn, the very first child to enter the world, the One who would make the world right.

You can hear the hope in Eve's words. Crushed by the weight of the fall, racked by guilt over her own deception yet clinging to the promise of redemption, perhaps she saw in this firstborn, the very first child to enter the world, the One who would make the world right. Of course, Eve couldn't know what God's plan to rescue the world would look like, how it would wind through sinful generations, would center on a single family who would then become a nation, from whom a single family again would bring forth a child from a humble and obscure young woman.

But alas, her Cain would not be the Promised One. He would live up to his name—*to get, to acquire, to grasp*[2]—in a way that she couldn't predict, as the seed of the serpent made its most immediate impact on this, her firstborn. Adam and Eve would experience in the first family the reality of sin's unwelcome gift to the human race: original sin.

✦ The Farmer and the Shepherd ✦

Cain was a farmer. Imagine how proud Adam must have been to have a son who picked up his vocation. God created humans, Genesis 2 says, in part to "work the ground." Imagine those days of Adam and Cain, working side by side turning over an earth that, while in a cosmos cursed by sin, laden with thorns and thistles that would make their work harder, still yielded beautiful flowers and luscious fruit. Farming is hard, laborious work. I wouldn't know it, having grown up in the suburbs where food comes to us on shelves at places like Walmart and Kroger. But those of you who work the ground like this, you know. Farming is the oldest vocation, made different with modern science and technology but still inescapably the product of blood and sweat. You can almost picture Adam and Cain in overalls.

The Bible presents a subtle contrast between Cain and his younger brother, Abel. We don't know how many other children Adam and Eve had, but these two are singled out in Genesis as a contrast between the way of the serpent and the way of God. While Cain labored in the fields, Abel tended livestock. Both vocations are presented as godly, worthy, honorable professions in Scripture. And there is some overlap between farmers and shepherds. Both tend to creation, both cultivating God's good creation, both working with dirt under their fingernails and sweat on their brows. The distinction between the brothers, though, seems to center on the nature of their souls. Abel is seen by New Testament writers as a man of faith (Heb. 11:4), whose humble worship was accepted by the Lord, while Cain is seen as a man full of hatred and disobedience toward God (1 John 3:12).

You wonder how he got this way. Was it a slow journey of rebellion? In some ways the text makes it seem so, with Jesus declaring Abel a martyr (Matt. 23). Perhaps Adam and Eve could see the painful seeds of Cain's journey away from God at an early age. Perhaps Abel was the good brother and friend who warned him. To be a martyr in Scripture is also to be a witness. Did Cain grow weary of his parents trying to bend his heart toward God? With no template, no other parents to consult, no bestselling books on behavior for insight, they had to rely on their parenting instincts and God's divine wisdom. Every parent can sympathize with a child who wants to go his or her own way.

> **You wonder how Cain got this way. Was it a slow journey of rebellion?**

The Bible skips Cain's childhood and picks up the action during the dramatic offering of worship, offered side by side, with his brother Abel. There are so many gaps in the narrative. Why did the two brothers offer a sacrifice at a different time than their parents? Was this a regular occurrence or an annual event? Though God had set an example in the animal sacrifice used to cover Adam and Eve's nakedness right after the fall, the pattern for such offerings was in the distant future, with a new people, and a whole new religious and legal paradigm.

There is much debate, as we discussed previously, as to why God rejected Cain's offering of the fruits he had cultivated from the ground and favored Abel's sacrifice of the best of his flocks. Perhaps God had given clear instructions, instructions not recorded by Moses, for a blood sacrifice. But we know that grain offerings would later be instituted by God as a form of worship. Or maybe God's rejection was based on Abel bringing "some of the firstborn of his flock" (Gen. 4:4) and Cain only bringing "some of the land's produce" (Gen. 4:3). Was this a difference in quality, with Abel offering God his first and best and Cain coming with halfhearted, leftover produce? I could make a pretty good sermon out of that thesis. I may start writing it now. But I'm not sure, either.

◆ The Heart of Cain ◆

What we can be sure of, what pulsates out of the text in Genesis, out of the passages in the New Testament (Matt. 23; Heb. 11–12; 1 John 3; Jude 11) is that God's rejection of Cain seems primarily directed not at Cain's sacrifice, but at Cain's heart. God has always been interested in the heart, even though the sacrifices were a way to model the idea of atonement and also the picture of gratitude, sacrificing our best for the Creator.

And yet approaching God with pride instead of humility is always a recipe for disaster, no matter how elaborate the good works. A phrase repeated in Scripture is that God "resists the proud, but offers grace to the humble" (James 4:6; 1 Peter 5:5 ; also see Prov. 3:34). The prophet Hosea, speaking for God to his people, declares: "For I desire faithful love and not sacrifice, the knowledge of God rather than burnt offerings" (Hos. 6:6). Jesus would later instruct the people of God leave the altar and repair a sinful separation with a brother (Matt. 5:24).

This is not to say that the sacrifice isn't important. It was vital. This altar was the way God met sinful people, before Jesus' atoning sacrifice tore the veil between humans and their Creator. But an empty ritual with an empty heart was an invitation for God's rejection.

Approaching God with pride is always a recipe for disaster.

We have to think this moment had been building for some time, perhaps years. Cain didn't just wake up on the wrong side of the bed or stumble over to the altar before having his morning coffee. This sacrifice was likely not the first time the brothers met God at the altar. We have this illusion that epic downfalls happen in an unguarded moment, the extramarital fling, the skimming off the top of the company books, the act of violence. But sin builds over time, encrusting itself, layer over layer on our hearts, unbothered by repentance.

This little baby, this "man sent from the Lord" had a dark soul and a cold heart, but perhaps he hid it well, behind the ritual sacrifices and a plastic smile. This entreaty by God, *sin lies at the door of your heart,* is God's diagnosis of a life marked by indifference to his Creator, a marked contrast to the humble faith of his brother, whom the writer of Hebrews calls righteous (Heb. 11:4).

Just listen to the way Cain responds after God accepts Abel's sacrifice and rejects his own. He's mad. He looks in the face of God, the God who could have struck his parents dead after they conspired with the serpent, who would one day flood the earth in judgment for evil, who once opened the earth and swallowed enemies of Moses. Yes, Cain has the hubris to raise his fingers to the heavens and tell God that God was wrong. This, of course, is the logical end of believing the lie whispered by Satan that to sin is to be like God.

This was a public confrontation between God and His creature, and a humiliating one at that. We don't know, but might imagine, that these sacrifices were celebrated family affairs, like a holiday with parents and siblings gathered. It's not clear how God signaled His acceptance and rejection. Did a fire consume Abel's sacrifice as happened in Elijah's showdown on Mt. Carmel (1 Kings 18), leaving Cain's bone-dry, the green shoots and grain lying there in the eerie quiet of God's silence?

Whatever form this rejection took, Cain's response was not one of contrition before a holy God. It was not the raw and humble prayer of David in Psalm 51, where the one caught in sin admitted his complicity before God and pleaded for forgiveness. Cain didn't even respond like Adam and Eve, who accepted the term of God's curse and their banishment from the Garden while continuing to worship and fear Elohim. Cain, Genesis tells us, was furious and despondent, his face falling.[3]

Sadness in the face of failure is not a sinful emotion, but this is not the kind of sorrow that the Bible says leads to repentance, but a "worldly grief [that] produces death" (2 Cor. 7:10). This was a devilish fury, the same poison carried by the snake that captivated his parents in the garden. This is Cain, drunk on the wine from the tree of knowledge of good and evil, declaring back to God what he thinks should be right and wrong. *How dare God tell me my sacrifice is wrong?*

Sound familiar? Oh, but it does. The created one rearranging the rules to accommodate his preferences. You can hear echoes of Cain's theology today in our age of pop spirituality. *The God I know wouldn't care about my lifestyle. The God I know wouldn't judge me for this.* Cain knows how to be true to himself.

◆ "I, the LORD, Search the Heart" ◆

And yet this story isn't really about Cain, but about the One who went searching for Adam in the garden, whispering with mercy, "Where are you?" Just as Jesus scrubbed the sore feet of and lifted bread to the lips of His betrayer in the upper room, just as God sent salvation to us "while we were yet sinners," so God responds to Cain, not with the snap of His fingers in judgment, but with small steps toward grace.

"Why are you furious?" God asks. "And why do you look despondent?" It reminds me of God's probing questions to His recalcitrant prophet Jonah, still smarting in rebellion and anger at God's removal of a plant. "Is it right for you to be angry?" God said to Jonah (Jonah 4:4).

God, we know, asks questions not in search of answers, but to lift away those layers that encase our souls. "I the LORD search the heart and test the mind," God says (Jer. 17:10 ESV). If Cain was willing, this confrontation by God could be a mirror to Cain's own soul. "If you do not do what is right, sin is crouching at the door."

In one sense, it's a piercing indictment. It's a red flag, a distress signal, a storm warning for the soul. In this moment, Cain could have seen the folly of his own way, could have knelt in repentance, could have turned toward God instead of away, to the wandering and destructive life he would live.

But alas, the sin crouching at the door is not just ignored, but is invited in, given a welcome mat, a guest room, and a hot shower. Kent Hughes says this was a stark choice for the wandering Son of Adam, "Cain stood at the edge of Hell. But sadly, God's graphic words about sin as a crouching beast bounced off his hardening heart, and in monumental willfulness he began his descent into the pit."[4]

I believe in God's sovereignty. God was not surprised by Cain's indifference. Heaven was not having to flip through the contingency plans for alternate scenarios. Still, while God doesn't wonder, we can. And imagine if this story had played out differently. What if Cain had repented?

I am reminded of the friend who, while looking up at an upside-down car wrapped around a telephone pole, glass embedded in his skull, finally realized this was the moment to turn in repentance toward God. I'm reminded of the son who, while sitting in a jail cell, decides to take seriously the faith of his father and joins rehab and begins a pathway toward freedom. I'm imagining another story told in these same Scriptures, where Jesus shares about another son who, having run far from his father, comes to the end of himself at the end of a pig trough.

We know how Cain's life turned out, but I can't help but plead with the prodigals who might, for some reason, have made their way to this chapter. Perhaps you think you are too far for grace. But know that the Father offers a way of escape. And I want to offer some comfort and hope to the parents who pray for prodigals, who like Adam and Eve, see their "child from the Lord" walk the wrong road. You can entrust your child to the Father who sees and loves and pursues.

♦ **Raging and Hating** ♦

Cain's anger was toward God, but his violence was committed against his brother. This is always how it is. Hating human beings is the most accessible way to rage at God. The apostle John would later write that hostility toward others is a sign that there is a breach in our relationship with God (1 John 4:20). You are mad at your spouse or your parents or your children or your boss or your neighbors, but you are really mad at the One who allowed those people to interrupt your life.

This was Cain and he nourished his hatred like a hobby. He watered its gardens and fed it fertilizer until hatred became a destructive weed that choked his soul. Here James is right, that sin, when it conceives, brings forth death. Yes, God was right. You will surely die, spiritually, physically, and in every way. Here is the tragic reality of our disobedience, the very first murder, in the very first family. The serpent was on the move and Cain was his chosen vessel.

Hating human beings is the most accessible way to rage at God.

Writing later in 1 John 3, the apostle John would use descriptive language to describe Cain's violence against Abel, with the original Greek meaning, "to slit the throat."[5] This was a defiant act against God in retaliation for his rejection of Cain's offering. *Blood sacrifice is what you accept; well, blood sacrifice is what you will have.*

John describes this brazen disobedience as "the way of Cain" and oh, how it is. Cain was the first to savagely kill another human in cold blood, but he would not be the last. Cain has too many heirs, many whose ambition to be like God led them to behave like animals, from Nebuchadnezzar to Nero, Herod to Hitler, and so many more. The way of Cain continues its bloody reign on our city streets, in the persecution of ethnic minorities in countries around the world, in abortion. It shows up, uninvited, in the wanton genocide of so many civil wars, in the sick trafficking of human beings around the world, in the murderous rampaging of terrorist networks. Sin was sold to Eve and is packaged today as the key to knowledge, the path to enlightenment. But the opposite is true, for sin really leads to this, one image-bearer with the blood of another image-bearer on his hands. Sin degrades and destroys.

In the eerie quiet after Cain snuffed out his brother's last breath, it must have seemed as if the serpent had won. You can almost hear his faint cackle in the distance, the high-fiving of hell while Cain offers a coldly indifferent response to the Lord's inquiry. "Am I my brother's keeper?"

It seems Satan is winning, as this spirit of "Am I My Brother's Keeper" echoes on in our casual looking away from bloodshed and violence, our blinking in the face of poverty and despair. God's reaction, however, is not one of indifference. The Almighty, who "does not slumber or sleep" (Ps. 121:4) saw that bloodshed in that field that day just as God would see the oppression of His people Israel (Ex. 3:7) and sees every single drop of innocent blood shed in the world. Abel's blood, God said, "cries out to me from the ground!" (Gen. 4:10).

"Though that blood was silent in the seared conscience of Cain," Charles Spurgeon wrote, "it had a voice elsewhere. A mysterious voice went up beyond the skies; it reached the ear of the invisible God and moved the heart of Eternal Justice."[6] The serpent didn't win. Sometimes the only salve, especially for those who live on the ragged margins of life, is to know that while the world may turn its comfortable eyes away, God sees. This reality, that God sees what nobody else sees, has motivated martyrs throughout history, has been the basis for the endurance of oppressed peoples who cling to this truth. This gave words to Fanny Crosby, who penned our richest hymns, and to the writers of African American spirituals, the testimony of those who walked by faith and not by sight. Because of a God who sees.

The ultimate act of God seeing, of the blood of injustice crying up to the Father, is the sight of another dead son of Eve, hideous and unrecognizable on a cruel Roman cross. This time, Jesus was the victim and, in assuming the punishment for the unpayable evil of human-kind, the guilty. In this one act, the One who was the perfect sacrifice approved by God, absorbed God's holy wrath against evil and turned back the curse that tempts humans to shed innocent blood. It's the first act in God's continuing justice, consumed in final victory at the end of the age. The way of Cain is reversed by the way of Jesus, who laid His life down for His brothers and sisters (Matt. 12:50), even while they are "still sinners" (Rom. 5:8). Sandra McCracken offers a word of hope:

> When fear and cynicism threaten to steal our joy—when we allow our consumption of bad news and media to overtake our participation in prayer—we need only to look to him and to sing back his own song of justice, to remember what he already accomplished on the cross. . . . Look for his compassion to rush into the places of disunity, war, and dissonance. While we may not have the power to fully defend and correct what is broken in the present, he is still God in our midst.[7]

God is still in our midst. And yet this knowledge can also be a terror. God saw Cain lift his hand against his brother in cold-blooded murder. *Cain, where are you?* Exposed, Cain stood alone, while God pronounces the curse:

> *"So now you are cursed, alienated from the ground that opened its mouth to receive your brother's blood you have shed. If you work the ground, it will never again give you its yield. You will be a restless wanderer on the earth." (Gen. 4:11–12)*

God comes calling. He sees. The sins we commit in darkened and unseen corridors. The vices we stuff into the closets of our souls, hoping they never escape. God's judgment struck at the heart of Cain's self-worship. His vocation, once the source of his identity and pride, would be closed to him. Having swallowed up Abel's blood, that soil that once nourished the crops Cain planted would now refuse Cain's plow.

"My punishment is too great to bear," Cain cries out, without true repentance or remorse. He's not sorry he sinned. He's not sorry that he broke the heart of his parents and slew his innocent brother in cold blood. He's not sorry that he played God and snuffed out the life of an image-bearer of the Almighty. Cain is after a reduced sentence, not a renewed heart. And yet you can't help but hear echoes of Calvary in this exchange with God.

> God is still in our midst. And yet this knowledge can also be a terror.

Jesus would absorb the curse for sin—cursed is everyone who hangs on a tree (Gal. 3:13; Deut. 21:23)—and it would be Jesus, the innocent one, who would bear a punishment that *only* He could bear. Every sinner, after all, every human being, stands like Cain, guilty before God, blood on our hands. We may not have physically killed our brothers, but according to God's law of love, the hatred we sow in our hearts is as good as murder. "Everyone who hates his brother or sister is a murderer, and you know that no murderer has eternal life residing in him" (1 John 3:15).

On our own, we face a just punishment from God that is "greater than we can bear." Sin, like a wave, crushes us. We have no escape and no hope and like Cain wander the earth in search of relief. Jesus offers an escape from punishment. This weight was put on His shoulders and we can become whole again.

◆ Marked and Watched ◆

Cain's response to God is interesting. He is chafing at God's judgment, but not expressing remorse or repentance. And then he says: "You are banishing me from the face of the earth, and I must hide from your presence" (Gen. 4:14), words, by the way, that God never said to him. God did say Cain would be a restless wanderer, but never "banished him from the face of the earth." And Cain's decision to hide from God's presence was a choice.

Cain didn't have to wander from the Almighty, who came calling for him in the midst of his sin. Cain chose separation from God because he refused to meet God on God's own terms. Like the rich young ruler in the Gospels, Cain went away sad because he loved his sin more than he wanted peace with God.

The entire message of Scripture, from Genesis to Revelation, is that you are separated from God because of your sin, but you don't have to stay that way. If you approach God in repentance and faith in His Son, Jesus Christ, you can have peace with God. You can know Him. Jesus would later say that he that "Whoever believes in the Son has eternal life; whoever does not obey the Son shall not see life, but the wrath of God remains on him" (John 3:36 ESV).

The Bible said that Cain turned away from Eden and went toward a place called Nod. I think there is significance here, not just a geographic footnote. And yet even as this prodigal packs his bags for the restless life without God, he asks God for one more request. In a weird way, he rejects God, but still needs Him, and pleads with God for protection from violence. He is worried that he will be a pariah, an outcast, and will be the victim of vigilante justice by his many siblings, who undoubtedly populate the earth at this time.

In one sense, this is more evidence of the way of Cain, a kind of myopic inability to see beyond his own self. The one who committed an egregious act of violence has somehow made himself the victim.

✦ Common Grace and the Mark of Cain ✦

And yet here is another window into the heart of God, grace even toward those who have turned their face away from Him. God could have struck Cain down dead, but instead Cain would be marked by God, in some mysterious way—a limp, a birthmark perhaps—that would protect him from the bloodthirsty vengeance of others. Theologians call this "common grace," a fancy way of describing how God provides for even those who reject Him. Jesus would explain this later by pointing to the provision of the sun and the rain:

> *For he causes his sun to rise on the evil and the good, and sends rain*
> *on the righteous and the unrighteous. (Matt. 5:45)*

Today people walk this earth under God's protection, without even acknowledging Him. They live in a world in which God is "sustaining all things by his powerful word" (Heb. 1:3). The sun rises and sets. The rains fall. They enjoy good health, good marriages, peace with neighbors—all due to the restraining power of the Holy Spirit and the providential grace of God.

The fact that Cain's life wasn't a tale of unmitigated disaster is because of God's common grace. Cain married and had children and his descendants, mostly pagans with no love for their Creator, nevertheless subdued God's good creation. Genesis tells us that it was Cain's family who were innovators and inventors, in crafts like metallurgy and music.

How is it that those who have set their face against God are able to find success in God's good world? It is because we have a gracious God who protects and empowers even sinners who are under His righteous wrath. "God restrains the full force of evil's power, by the ordering of societies, by the provision of governments, and by the refreshment of culture," writes David Atkinson, "God is concerned with the growth of art, of society, of technology even in a world which is homesick for him; even for people who are out of touch with his love. The sons of Cain, too, have gifts from God."[8]

Common grace is why your unbelieving doctor might be amazingly good at what he does, why you don't have to ask if your airline pilot is a Christian, why some of the best artists are pagans. "The earth and everything in it, the world and its inhabitants, belong to the LORD" (Ps. 24:1), writes the psalmist. This big wide world and everything in it is God's and even the beautiful and artistic works of those who don't acknowledge God bring glory back to Him.

✦ Building a City, Losing a Soul ✦

What became of Cain? Where did his restless wandering take him? The Bible says that Cain built a city named after his son Enoch. It is perhaps the world's first city. His would be a family of builders and inventors—and yet this progress came at a cost. You don't have to read too far into his genealogy to see that Cain left no legacy of faith. As their society progressed, so did their sin.

Moses parallels the family of Cain and the family of Seth, who would be another of Adam and Eve's children. We will talk later about the cosmic implications of these two dueling seeds, one the seed of the serpent, one the seed out of whom the Messiah would eventually be birthed.

But I want to close this chapter by thinking about the sad legacy of Cain, the one who bore the mark of God's grace. Cain built a city and lost his soul. In Cain's story we hear echoes of the cynicism of the writer of Ecclesiastes, decrying the empty pursuits of fame and fortune.

This isn't to say that progress is bad. In fact, as we have seen, this is what image-bearers do. We take the raw materials of God's good creation and build. We create. We innovate. And yet there is a kind of ambition that promises happiness apart from God. To wander away from God and find your worth in what you build, only to get to the end of your life and discover the meaninglessness of self-worship, is such a tragic story, told again and again in every generation. I've read the painful biographies of superstar athletes and famous musicians and wealthy CEOs who admit their spiritual emptiness. There is a restlessness, like Cain's, that prevents them from finding rest in God.

Jesus understood this deep soul hunger. To the woman at the well, stuck on the treadmill of relationships, He said there was a living water that would quench that deep thirst. To the wandering souls who, like Cain, ask, "How can I possibly bear the weight of my guilt?" Jesus says that there is a better way than to gain the whole world and lose our souls. We can be found again by coming home, home to the One who offers to bear the weight of our guilt.

The Conquering Seed

Seth, Enoch, Lamech, and the Promise of God

Rise, the woman's conquering seed,
Bruise in us the serpent's head.
Now display thy saving power,
Ruined nature now restore. . . .[1]

—CHARLES WESLEY

I'm writing this chapter on the very last day of July. The temperature will rise to above 90 as we enter what looks to be a scorching August. And yet I'm thinking about Christmas. No, it's not that I'm nostalgic for that time of year when the lights dim and the music plays, when we gather to think about the incarnation of the Son of God. Well, maybe I am a little nostalgic about that. But I'm thinking about Christmas because the very beginning of the Bible, the book of Genesis and the start of human civilization, has a lot to do with Christmas, and with the end of the world we read about in Revelation.

But I'm not actually talking about Christmas as we commonly know it—the majestic story told in the Gospels of shepherds and wise men and angels, and an impoverished Jewish couple entrusted with the care of the Son of God. I'm talking about the epic battle waged behind the scenes, the spiritual warfare between God and Satan that climaxes in the birth of Jesus described in the book of Revelation:

> *A great sign appeared in heaven: a woman clothed with the sun, with the moon under her feet and a crown of twelve stars on her head. She was pregnant and cried out in labor and agony as she was about to give birth. Then another sign appeared in heaven: There was a great fiery red dragon having seven heads and ten horns, and on its heads were seven crowns. Its tail swept away a third of the stars in heaven and hurled them to the earth. And the dragon stood in front of the woman who was about to give birth, so that when she did give birth it might devour her child. She gave birth to a Son, a male who is going to rule all nations with an iron rod. Her child was caught up to God and to his throne. The woman fled into the wilderness, where she had a place prepared by God, to be nourished there for 1,260 days. (Rev. 12:1–6)*

We typically don't think of Christmas in these terms.[2] This certainly wasn't a silent night, a cozy Hallmark holiday. And yet this apocalyptic vision in the last book of the Bible helps us understand what is going on here in this first book of the Bible.

✦ A Boring List of Names? ✦

This is what Moses is writing, to the people of Israel who would read his words, and to us, the people of God reading many centuries later, after that baby was born to Mary, after the cross, after the resurrection and the coming of the Holy Spirit. This is what is taking place in what seems like a boring list of names in Genesis, the section of Scripture we are most likely to skip as we make our way through the Bible.

The story of creation and the characters that inhabit this very first book are not just offering bland morality tales. The Bible is not just a disconnected series of narrative and wisdom and letters, but a cohesive story of what is really going on in the world. It's a story of God's rescue of His creation, of God's saving of His people, and of God triumphing over the enemy.

After Adam and Eve were caught red-handed, God announced His judgment and how the world would be different because of the entrance of sin. In the midst of this crushing punishment, the Creator inserted a sliver of grace, a prophecy that frames the rest of Scripture:

> *I will put hostility between you and the woman, and between your offspring and her offspring. He will strike your head, and you will strike his heel. (Gen. 3:15)*

If this promise from God—ongoing warfare between the seed of the serpent and the seed of the woman, with God delivering a final crushing blow to the enemy of our souls—is the beginning of the story, Revelation gives us a peek at how the story ends. It is this lens, then, that should frame the way we read Genesis, and especially those lists of names we want to skip. Because in these names are not just the stories of men like Lamech and Seth, Enoch and Jubal, but the story of God's sovereign work in the world. Two parallel family trees, one the seed of the serpent, the other, God's righteous remnant. It's a paradox, both the manifestation of the human race's dalliance with death and the promise of new life in each new generation, both "and he died, and he died" and "he fathered a son, in his likeness, according to his image."

Scholar Kenneth Matthews writes: "The ongoing tension between the blessing of the imago Dei and the unlawful attempt of humanity to achieve more than God intended is the theological undercurrent of the genealogy."[3]

♦ Going the Way of Cain ♦

We saw in the last chapter Cain's continued rejection of God's offers of grace—first in refusing to repent after thumbing his nose at God; and then again showing a stunning lack of contrition upon killing his own brother in cold blood. Cain could have, should have, been struck dead by God on the spot, but instead God promised to protect Cain from vigilante justice while he wandered further and further away from the One who made him.

Two parallel family trees, one the seed of the serpent, the other, God's righteous remnant.

Moses tells us that Cain became the builder of a city, a city named after his son Enoch. I'm not sure there is anything nefarious we can ascribe to Cain's city building and naming it after his son. But as the generations unfold in his family, it's hard not to notice the glaring omission of their acknowledgment of God. I'm not saying Cain should have named the very first city Elohim, but there is no record of worship, of turning their hearts toward their Creator. In a sense Cain and his succeeding generations were a fulfillment of the desire to be "all-knowing" without knowing the source of that knowledge.

And yet we shouldn't look at Cain building a city and conclude that cities are bad. In fact, the narrative of Scripture, the direction the

Bible points humanity toward, is from an undeveloped garden to a city, whose "architect and maker is God" (Heb. 11:10). God is not against technological progress. Cain's offspring were known for their inventiveness. So many things we consider normal to our everyday lives were invented in this age:

- Jabal is "the first of the nomadic herdsmen" (Gen. 4:20). He essentially invented the raising of livestock. So, if you are a cattle rancher or a cowboy or just someone who likes burgers, Jabal is your guy.
- Jabal's brother Jubal is "the first of all who play the lyre and flute" (Gen. 4:21). He basically invented musical instruments. So if you are in the worship band at church, thank Jubal.
- Tubal-cain is "who made all kinds of bronze and iron tools" (Gen. 4:22). This guy was one of the first known metal workers! So I'm thankful for him as I type on my MacBook Pro and look out the window at my Ford F-150.

Cain's family was inventive. As we've already discussed, this is a sign of God's common grace, giving gifts even to a family that had turned their back on God. These are God's image-bearers fulfilling the creation mandate to subdue the earth without even really knowing why they are subduing it. It's a testament to God-endowed, human ingenuity. I think it's also a bit of a corrective to our age, where we assume that people not born in our generation are not as enlightened as we are.

I remember, for instance, touring the pyramids in Egypt several years ago, amazing wonders built by pagan kings over five thousand years ago. Modern architects and engineers still marvel at how those ancient communities were able to build such marvelous structures. We too often assume that we are the smart ones and that people who lived in earlier moments in human history were somehow ignorant or incapable.

One scholar, John Walton, attributes the inventiveness of Cain to the curse. Forced to find another way to live besides farming, wandering and restless, Cain and his offspring found alternate ways to survive:

> Is there any significance to city-building and technological development being linked to the line of Cain? Perhaps no more than to demonstrate the time-honored maxim that necessity is the mother of invention. Because Cain and his family were forced to their extremities, they could only survive by means of human advancement. There is nothing to reflect rebellion here, only an indication that even Cain's line continues to enjoy the blessing by subduing and ruling.[4]

And yet it was not only the "subduing and ruling" that progressed, but the downward spiral into sensuality and violence. One glaring example is one of Cain's descendants, Lamech. Genesis records perhaps one of the earliest poems in human history, a macabre ode to sin and depravity:

> *Lamech said to his wives:*
>
> > *Adah and Zillah, hear my voice;*
> > *wives of Lamech, pay attention to my words.*
> > *For I killed a man for wounding me,*
> > *a young man for striking me.*
> > *If Cain is to be avenged seven times over,*
> > *then for Lamech it will be seventy-seven times! (Gen. 4:23–24)*

This is a son of Cain living out the way of Cain, the seed of the serpent exulting in his direct opposition to God. Whereas Cain offered sacrifices and complained about being away from the presence of God, this generation is open about its flagrant sin. And please notice that this begins with a violation of God's design for the family. Lamech took two wives.

To Adam and Eve, God said, "This is why a man leaves his mother and father and bonds with his wife, and they become one flesh" (Gen. 2:24), a command repeated by Jesus (Matt. 19:5) and Paul (Eph. 5:31). It's no coincidence that his celebration of sexual license is the fruit of a family and a people who have rejected God. And it's not coincidence that the denial of God's law when it comes to the family runs side by side with rejection of God's law in the celebration of violence. In this, Lamech represents what sin really is—a distortion of God's good gifts. The beauty of sexual expression within marriage is distorted for personal pleasure and exploitation, and the wonder of innovation in metals is used to make weapons of war and commit violence.[5]

This is truly what it means to live "the way of Cain" instead of the way of God, to follow the serpent into trying to be like God instead of living in obedience to God, to use God's good gifts against Him. And it sounds so eerily familiar to our modern times, where we consider ourselves so enlightened. We, like Cain's offspring, pride ourselves on our modern inventions while celebrating sexual license and glorifying violence. Sin is often marketed as progress, and yet these patterns are the oldest habits in the world. The writer of Ecclesiastes is right when he says that there "nothing new under the sun" (Eccl. 1:9). "Cain's family," Derek Kidner says, "is a microcosm: its pattern of technical prowess and moral failure is that of humanity."[6]

✦ A Righteous Remnant ✦

In 1994, Major League Baseball went on strike. This meant that the players who usually made up the rosters of the big-league teams sat out and replacement players were paid to play baseball. Eventually the owners and the players worked out their differences, and the professionals came back, replacing the plumbers and accountants and weekend warriors in the field.

This is typically what we think when we think of the biblical character Seth. And the text of Scripture seems to indicate this. At the end of Genesis 4, Moses almost seems to write of Seth's birth this way:

> *Adam was intimate with his wife again, and she gave birth to a son and named him Seth, for she said, "God has given me another offspring in place of Abel, since Cain killed him." A son was born to Seth also, and he named him Enosh. At that time people began to call on the name of the* Lord. *(Gen. 4:25–26)*

God has given me another offspring in place of Abel, since Cain killed him. In some ways, the name Seth can mean "substitute."[7] And yet there can also be a deeper meaning to this son, born to replace a son who was lost. Augustine believed Seth's name meant "resurrection."[8] I think this, too, is what Moses is getting at, especially as he begins chapter 5, which opens like this:

> *This is the document containing the family records of Adam. On the day that God created man, he made him in the likeness of God; he created them male and female. When they were created, he blessed them and called them mankind.*
>
> *Adam was 130 years old when he fathered a son in his likeness,*

according to his image, and named him Seth. Adam lived 800 years
after he fathered Seth, and he fathered other sons and daughters. So
Adam's life lasted 930 years; then he died. (Gen. 5:1–5)

Here, in the wake of the tragedy of Cain's sin and the tragedy
of Cain's family line, a compounding story of sin and depravity, the
people of God are reminded that while the seed of the serpent grows,
so too will the seed of the woman, that God is preserving a righteous
remnant, a people from whom will come the promise and the rescue
of the world. Scholar Mitchell Chase writes:

> In one sense, God appointed Seth to the stage of history by bringing
> him into the world through the woman. In another sense, the birth
> of Seth is the reversal of the death Eve endured with Abel's murder.
> Seth's birth is a reversal of death not because Seth is Abel reincarnate,
> nor because someone was raised bodily from the dead, but because
> the *promised seed* experienced a death when Abel was murdered, and
> now the family line of promise and hope can continue because God
> granted Eve another son. The line lived again.[9]

Moses reminds us here in chapter 5, as sin makes its way around
the world, as it marbles itself into the human experience, as depravity
and violence and sensuality begin to define God's good creation, that
He has not given up on the human project. Moses reminds us here
that still, in the midst of all this, that human beings are still created in
God's image, and that His plan is not thwarted by the enemy. What's
more, he reminds us that it is through men and women coming together in marriage and through families that His promise of redemption will march through the ages.

Even in a fallen world, even against the backdrop of sensuality and sin, God's design for human flourishing didn't change. Pastor Tony Evans says that "family was established to provide the opportunity and framework for individuals to collectively carry out the plan of God in history. In particular, that plan includes the replication of God's image and the implementation of His rule, or *dominion*, on earth. Dominion simply means ruling on God's behalf in history so that history comes under God's authority."[10]

This doesn't mean, of course, that those whom God has not called to be married are somehow inferior or incomplete or less important to the mission of God. In Christ, we are a new family with a new identity. And yet regardless of our family status, we can affirm and uphold God's design for marriage between men and women and the raising of children in a way that images and points forward to Christ's love for His church (Eph. 5).

This declaration by God that His plan for His image-bearers is still in effect should also shape the way we see the world, that even in a fallen age, sinful humans have value and worth. There is nothing of the image of God that is lost, even after the fall. We see this later in Genesis 9, after God reiterates the value of human life and even way ahead in James 3 as Jesus' brother appeals to human dignity as a way of urging God's people toward kindness and respect.

It can be difficult to see humanity as image-bearers, in a world so filled with sin, so fraught with division, a world that so cheapens life that it seems the way of God and the promises of God are no longer in effect. But a word of hope at the end of the tale of Cain's family echoes God's words in Genesis 4:26: "At that time people began to call upon the name of the LORD." And Genesis 5 unfolds this hope: that God's promise of deliverance will endure.

In this way Seth's unique birth images Jesus as both a "replacement," the substitute who would take the place of those dead in their sins and as resurrection, who would defeat sin, death, and the grave.

This is the purpose, I believe, of Moses pairing Genesis 4, with its vivid description of the fulfillment of the curse of sin, and Genesis 5, with its elevation of the faithful witness of Seth's descendants. This is evident even in the way prominent members of both Cain and Seth are contrasted,

> There is nothing of the image of God that is lost, even after the fall.

so much so that some of the names in each genealogy are the same. There is an Enoch in Cain's family and an Enoch in Seth's family; a wicked Lamech descended from Cain and a righteous Lamech who longs for his son, Noah, to do great things; and not one, but two Methuselahs, one of whom lived 969 years (a trivia answer I always aced in Sunday school)!

✦ The Deepest Obedience ✦

Enoch, the righteous one, the seventh son of Seth, appears on the scene with some mystery. Jude tells us Enoch was a preacher of righteousness, an early prophet who warned of sin and God's judgment (Jude 1:14). Moses tells us in Genesis that Enoch didn't die but "walked with God: and he was not" (Gen. 5:24 KJV). The writer of Hebrews says that because of his faith, he didn't suffer death (Heb. 11:5). Enoch was someone who walked with God in a time when walking with God was countercultural. His life, says Kent Hughes, "indicates the deepest obedience."[11] Charles Spurgeon said of Enoch's faith, "It was not that he merely thought of God, that he speculated about God, that he argued about God, that he read about God, that he talked about God; he walked with God, which is the practical and experimental part of true godliness."[12]

Enoch walked with God for three hundred years and then was delivered to heaven. In many ways, he is a shadow of the unfolding of God's mysterious plan of redemption, a pre-figuring of redemption and resurrection. Jesus would later experience death and defeat it, so that by faith we too might not have to suffer eternal death. We, who believe in the promise of God, are like Enoch. We walk with God and we will one day be resurrected to new life.

This section of Genesis was written on purpose to the children of God to get them to see the contrast between the seed of the serpent and the seed of the woman, between the way of the wicked and the way of God. Later, Psalm 1 contrasts the way of the wicked and the way of the righteous. The purpose of God calling out Israel was to be a contrast, a difference, from the way of the pagan nations. "Be holy as I am holy" is to say, "Be other, be different, live the way of Seth instead of the way of Cain."

Jesus would condemn the religious leaders, who assumed they were the good people, and said that their outward acts of righteousness were no cover for their inward wickedness. Mincing no words, He said, "You are of your father the devil." You are a son of Cain. The book of Ephesians says that this is the natural way of humans, that we are children of disobedience who take their marching orders from "the ruler of the power of the air." Romans says that "there is no one righteous, not even one." We are Sons of Cain, children of the devil. Hard words.

The promise of God, though, is that while evil seems to dominate and it appears that the devil keeps winning, God is always at work calling out a people. Out of this people came the second Adam, the One who redeems sons of Cain and makes them children of God.

✦ Which Way? ✦

These two paths are the choice today, for every person. You can follow your heart or "do it my way" or "live your own truth" and find material success, perhaps even some temporary flourishing, but in the end, the way of Cain leads to hell. "There is a way that seems right to a person," Proverbs tells us, "but its end is the way to death." Spiritual and physical death. Death of relationships. Death of our spiritual lives. Death to the relationship with the One who created us.

Or you can follow the way of Seth, the way of David, the way of King Jesus, who saves us from enslavement to ourselves.

"Behold what manner of love," John writes, "that *we* should be called children of God" (emphasis mine). The apostle John is writing to the church, marveling that we wicked, sinful, corrupted sons of Cain can be redeemed and adopted into the family of God as sons of God. God is creating in Christ, a new family, a new people, a righteous seed who will rule and reign and subdue the earth without thorns and thistles, who will live in happiness and harmony in this garden turned city, where there is no death or pain or sadness.

This titanic struggle, the war between the seed of the woman and the seed of the serpent, is the ongoing struggle throughout human history, and it rages today. Though Satan was defeated at the cross when Jesus whispered the words, "It is finished," and is a defeated, toothless lion, he and his demon horde attack and wage war on God's people. The enemy preys on our sinful lusts and temptations, he instills fear and doubt in the hearts of God's people, he distracts us with worldly lusts and deadening comfort. But we should not despair, for even in these early pages of His Word, God shows us that while the way of Cain seems to flourish with depravity and wickedness, the way of Seth, the way of David, the way of Jesus endures and that one day that wicked beast will be put in hell forever, to "no longer deceive the nations."

Until then, even those who have turned from their idols and have put their faith in Christ as Lord still can feel the pull of the way of Cain. You may be a child of God, adopted as a Son of God with all the rights and privileges of sonship, but the devil still wants to pull you back into living like a son or daughter of Cain. The world system is empowered by Satan and ruled by sons and daughters of Cain.

But if you are in Christ, you are not a son or daughter of Cain. You belong to God's righteous remnant. I just love this word from Old Testament scholar Sandra Richter, who reminds us:

> Thus, when you said, "yes" to God at that altar rail years ago, or last week as you knelt at the side of your bed, what you were doing was "undoing" the choice of Adam in your life. Whereas Adam said "no" to the sovereignty of God, you said "yes." What is the prayer? "Jesus be *lord* of my life."
>
> . . . In sum, in the work of Christ, the rebellious heart is softened, the choice is "unmade," the broken relationship is healed, the curse is lifted, and the lost inheritance regained. All this because the second time around, Adam did not fail.[13]

You are a son or daughter of the king. You are a new creation. You have God's spirit within you. But it's a fight. Paul tells us to put on

God's full armor, to equip ourselves with the truth of God's Word and the reality of who we are in Christ.

One day, not too long from now, that fight will be over. One day the beast will be locked up forever where he belongs. One day we will experience the fullness of our adoption in Christ, the fullness of our new creation reality, the fullness of what we were truly made to be. That old Adam, the way of Cain, will be put off forever.

The Depraved

The Mysterious Madness of the Nephilim

*But what we see here is that evil has multiplied faster than the
population, so that it has spread through the entire people of earth.
Man was beyond self-help. Demonic powers were in the driver's seat.*[1]

R. KENT HUGHES

They may the most peculiar creatures in the Bible and we are not
even sure what they really are. They've been featured in literature
for thousands of years and popularized in culture. The Nephilim have
made appearances in *The X-Files*, *Shadowhunters*, and *Noah*. Video
games like *El Shaddai*, *Tomb Raider*, and *Payday 2* feature Nephilim,
as does literature such as *House of Night*, *Fallen*, and *Atlas Shrugged*.

What's more, since the dawn of time, humans have imagined, in
their legends and myths, a kind of half-man, half-god figure, from the
Babylonian Gilgamesh to the demigods of Greek mythology. But who
are these strange characters who make their way onto the pages of our
Bibles, who appear during a time of a downward descent into human
depravity, a period described by Moses as "every inclination of the
human mind was nothing but evil all the time" (Gen. 6:5)?

The answer is, well . . . complicated.

✦ Half Man, Half God? Can It Be? ✦
Two Theories from History

So have you turned your Bible to Genesis 6 and asked yourself what in the world is going on? It turns out that you are not alone. What if I told you that Christians have wrestled with this story from Genesis for all of church history and that faithful scholars and Bible teachers find themselves on two sides and hold their positions with little certainty? As of this writing, I am not sure where I land, but I do think whoever the Nephilim are, whoever the sons of God are, God's larger purpose is communicating to us the depravity of human beings, how mankind's dalliance with the devil produced just what God predicted it would: sin and death.

Let's begin by reading the text from Genesis 6:

When mankind began to multiply on the earth and daughters were born to them, the sons of God saw that the daughters of mankind were beautiful, and they took any they chose as wives for themselves. And the LORD *said, "My Spirit will not remain with mankind forever, because they are corrupt. Their days will be 120 years." The Nephilim were on the earth both in those days and afterward, when the sons of God came to the daughters of mankind, who bore children to them. They were the powerful men of old, the famous men. (Gen. 6:1–4)*

Historically, the Christian church has held one of two positions. The first position is held by many of the church fathers such as Ambrose, Tertullian, Cyprian, and Clement of Alexandria.[2] Many Jewish scholars also held this view.[3]

This view argues that the term "sons of God" here in Genesis refers to fallen angels having illicit sexual relationships with human women. One of the more compelling reasons is because the normative usage of this term, "sons of God," is to refer to angels (Job 1:6; 2:1; 38:7; Ps. 29:1, 89:7; Dan. 3:25).[4] It also seems that the New Testament writers Peter and Jude refer to this:

> *For if God didn't spare the angels who sinned but cast them into hell and delivered them in chains of utter darkness to be kept for judgment; and if he didn't spare the ancient world, but protected Noah, a preacher of righteousness, and seven others, when he brought the flood on the world of the ungodly. (2 Peter 2:4–5)*

> *The angels who did not keep their own position but abandoned their proper dwelling, he has kept in eternal chains in deep darkness for the judgment on the great day. (Jude 1:6)*

Peter and Jude are still somewhat ambiguous, but the idea of "angels who sinned" and the judgment of Noah's flood in the same sentence, seems to point back to Genesis 6 and relationship between the sons of God and daughters of men. In this view, the wickedness between angels and humans was so great it required God to cleanse the earth with the flood and lock up these fallen angels until the time of judgment.

This fits with a key theme of Genesis, of God's gracious provision and human's exploitation of that provision and grasping for power and godlike abilities that actually make him behave in less human ways. This is the same problem we see in Genesis 11, where humans attempt to "reach God" by building the tower of Babel. It's a participation in the Genesis 3 lie of the serpent that "you can be like God."

It is hard for us to imagine fallen angels cohabitating with humans and creating these warlike, depraved evil monsters, but that could also just be because our minds, in this secular age, do not think of the super-natural and the ways in which demonic powers might prey on God's people. Throughout Scripture, we see angels take on human bodies and human characteristics (Matt. 8:28–34). Even craving human bodies. This is the height of human depravity.

There is another way that Christians have read Genesis 6 through-out the ages, one shared by Augustine and by reformers John Calvin[5] and Martin Luther.[6] For this view, Jesus' explicit teaching that angels neither "marry nor are given in marriage" makes it seem impossible for angels to procreate (Matt. 22:30). What's more, there are instances in Scripture where the term "sons of God" is used to refer to human beings (Hos. 1:10). Seeing the sons of God as the descendants of Seth weaves Genesis 6 into the context of the entire book of Genesis, with the promise of Genesis 3:15 and the seed of the serpent and seed of the woman playing out in the dual genealogies of Seth and Cain—as we have already seen.

> Our minds, in this secular age, do not think of the supernatural and the ways in which demonic powers might prey on God's people.

Genesis 6 seems to be the climax of this battle, where even the righteous line is over-taken by the depravity of the unrighteous. Sons of God could refer to Seth's righteous line intermarrying with the daughters of the heathen Cainites. Some even read Genesis 6, which says "they took any they chose" as wives, as referring to the sexual perversion of Lamech in Genesis 4, who took multiple wives for himself.

Those who see the "sons of God" as the family of Seth rightly see this as a trajectory of the Old Testament, that even the most righteous are inevitably corrupted and must be saved. Throughout Israel's history, they gave in to the temptation to intermingle with the pagan nations, blurring their witness and abandoning God for false idols. God's people were not to intermarry with the pagan nations, but were to be distinct, a light to the nations that pointed to Yahweh. It is a stark warning for the people of God in every age that we too easily become enamored with a worldly system that is opposed to God. We can, as Jesus said, be salt that "loses its saltiness" (Matt. 5:13 NIV). "What does light have to do with darkness?" Paul warned the Corinthian church (1 Cor. 6:14–17). The growing perversion, even among the righteous line of Seth, even among those whom had just begun "to call on the name of the LORD" (Gen. 4:26), would fit with a theme in Scripture of a falling away of God's people as the judgment of God grows closer. In his last letter to Timothy, Paul warned:

> *For the time will come when people will not tolerate sound doctrine, but according to their own desires, will multiply teachers for themselves because they have an itch to hear what they want to hear. They will turn away from hearing the truth and will turn aside to myths. (2 Tim. 4:3–4)*

It's not hard to see that trend in our own day, especially among churches in affluent, Western countries. We are too easily tempted toward worldliness and held captive by false ideologies.

◆ So Who Are They and Why Does It Matter? ◆

So, what, exactly, are the Nephilim? Are these mysterious creatures related to the Sons of God and the daughters of women? Are they incidental to them? Are they the raging rock-monster half-devil off-spring of an illicit relationship between angels and humans? There are multiple theories here. Most who hold that the "sons of God" in Genesis 6 are angels hold that the Nephilim are their offspring. The word *Nephilim* has an obscure meaning. It can mean "fallen ones," but was also translated by early Greek translators of the Septuagint (the Bible read in Second Temple era and the Bible Jesus and the apostles read) as "giants."[7]

What's even more mysterious about the Nephilim is that it doesn't appear they were wiped off the face of the earth in the flood. Genesis 6:4 says, "The Nephilim were on the earth both in those days and afterward." And they show up in a few more places in the story of Israel, such as when the spies returned to give a report to Moses, the pessimistic, unbelieving ten spies. "We even saw the Nephilim there—the descendants of Anak come from the Nephilim!" (Num. 13:33) they reported. It could be that these spies were exaggerating. *These warriors there are huge, they are giants, they are . . . like Nephilim!* But later in Deuteronomy, Moses confirmed the existence of these rather large creatures (Deut. 1:28; 2:10). And in Deuteronomy 3:11, Israel is said to have defeated Og of Bashan, the last of "what was left of the remnant of the Rephaim." Some have even linked the Nephilim to the giants in the land driven out by Joshua and even to Goliath, perhaps the remaining of the Nephilim seed.[8]

All of this, of course, is obscure and hard to make sense of. As of this writing, I'm not even sure where I land. On the one hand, it's hard for me to imagine the idea of fallen angels having relations with human women and bearing half-human/half-angel sort of devilish supervillains. It raises all kinds of questions. Can humans give birth to anything but more image-bearers? Can angels procreate? Scripture seems to indicate that these things are outside of what God allows in creation, though it is not completely clear. And the "sons of God" representing the line of Seth, of whom it is said, "[they] began to call upon the name of the Lord," and the daughters of men representing the line of Cain, seems to fit with the overall thrust and direction of Genesis.

And yet I can't escape the fact that a plain reading of that text seems to indicate something supernatural and nefarious is going on here, and the texts in Jude and 2 Peter seem to point both to God's judgment of humans for their escalating depravity and to the fallen angel host for its preying on humans.

What's more, we live in a very materialistic world. It's hard to wrap our minds around this strange mixing of the human and supernatural. However, these kinds of myths have been around since the beginning. According to scholar Gordon Wenham, "Stories of superhuman demigods like Gilgamesh were commonplace, and intercourse with the divine was regularly sought in the fertility cults of Canaan and the sacred marriage rites of Mesopotamia."[9] And these myths and legends continue on through history, from the demigods of Greek mythology to our own modern pop culture and literary imagination of the divine and supernatural. Could it be that the enemy impregnated humans in order to create a devilish copycat of what is to come, fully human, fully divine, perfect God in the flesh in Jesus Christ?

None of us can be too sure of exactly how to interpret this text. But whether you think the sons of God are angels or descendants of Seth, whether you think the Nephilim are just really big and hairy warriors or superhuman devils, we can be sure that what God is trying to communicate are two important lessons: humans left to their own devices descend into chaos, depravity, and wickedness; and we need a Savior, a righteous seed, the God-man to come and rescue us from ourselves.

❖ Coming Judgment and Overwhelming Grace ❖

In a way, the two most common theories of the Nephilim and the sons of God can both offer important lessons for those of us who read Genesis. Beyond our fascination, when we've put down the commentaries and Hebrew texts and have stopped Googling Genesis 6, we should allow God's Word to speak to us what God intended.

First, it is clear in Genesis that there have always been two groups of people, those who fear God and those who rebel, those who live the way of Seth and those who live the way of Cain, the righteous and the unrighteous. This is the epic clash throughout history that Genesis 3:15 predicted. Regardless of how you interpret Genesis 6, it is clear that even the good seed, the righteous remnant, is being corrupted. Consider that only Noah's family, by the time of God's judgment, was found with faith, as we will see later.

Even the good seed was corrupted. This is the story of the Old Testament: even the best and the brightest are not enough to save humanity. Not Seth. Not Enoch. Not even Noah, who after the flood fell into sin. Not even Abraham, who lied about his wife and had a child with his servant. Not even David, who exploited Bathsheba and murdered her husband. Not even Jacob, a deceiver. Not even Hezekiah, whose life ended in disgrace, as did Gideon's. Samson, the strongman, saved Israel from the Philistines, but couldn't save himself.

Failure is the story of God's people in the Old Testament, and it's our story as well. Even the best of us fall short. Isaiah 53:6 says that at the end of the day, we are all going the way of Cain, we "all went astray," while Romans 3:10 says that there is "no one righteous, not even one."

We need someone from the righteous "branch," a son of Eve, a son of David, who is also a Son of God. This is the case that the New Testament makes—that Jesus of Nazareth is that One, of whom the Father said, "This is my beloved Son, with whom I am well-pleased." The One who endured temptation, went to the cross, and with His life and death saves humanity and saves the cosmos. The most important lesson from Genesis 6 is not identifying the Nephilim, but identifying the state of our own souls, to look up and put our faith in God's salvation before we face the time of God's judgment, to recognize that we cannot save ourselves.

> **Failure is the story of God's people in the Old Testament, and it's our story as well.**

The state of the human heart in these times was desperate. Moses says that in those days, "every inclination of the human mind was nothing but evil all the time" (Gen. 6:5). And yet the indictment against Noah's age is an indictment of our age. This is what Jesus said: "As the days of Noah were, so the coming of the Son of Man will be" (Matt. 24:37). The prophet Jeremiah diagnoses the true nature of the human heart as "more deceitful than anything else" (Jer. 17:9), while Paul soberly reminds us that without a supernatural rescue by God, we are "dead in [our] trespasses and sins" (Eph. 2:1–3).

Thankfully, we have in Christ the perfect son of Eve, the second Adam, the only one from the line of Seth who could absorb the judgment of God, who "while we were still sinners . . . died for us" (Rom. 5:8). Jesus came to die for the depraved.

And yet the mysterious nature of the Nephilim and the sons of God should also be a somber warning that our struggle for faith is not merely a human struggle. Satan did not take the curse from God in Eden lying down. Satan and his demon horde would strike again and again, throughout the story of Israel, in the life of Christ, both as tempter and murderer, to work against God's rescue of His fallen race. And today, though he has been defeated, he will do what he can to thwart God's plans. Though his sentence was pronounced in Jesus' words on the cross—"It is finished" (John 19:30)—Satan still roams around, seeking whom he may devour (1 Peter 5:8). This titanic struggle is against "the rulers, the authorities, against the cosmic powers of this darkness, against evil, spiritual forces in the heavens" (Eph. 6:12).

As Christians who have put our faith in God's rescue of us from our own sinfulness, we can defeat Satan because we stand in the victory God has already secured. We can pray against the powers of hell. We can arm ourselves with the truth. We don't need to fear superhuman devil creatures like the Nephilim, we don't need to fear the underworld of spiritual warfare, because in the power of the Spirit of the one who has crushed the serpent, we are "more than conquerors" (Rom. 8:37).

CHAPTER EIGHT

The Preacher

Noah's Lonely Courage, and a Flood That Saves

It is always that way for God's people. Athanasius stood alone.
Luther stood alone. Knox stood alone. In their day they were
ridiculed, threatened, sometimes even persecuted for their beliefs.
But they triumphed because they believed God, whose word is
never shaken.[1]

—JAMES MONTGOMERY BOICE

It is a bit strange, really, that the Genesis flood has been told as an adorable kids' story. I mean, can you find a church nursery not adorned with the kind of smiling, lovable Noah, flanked by chubby animals, blithely waving from the deck of a boat sort of cruising on the water?

Weirdly, we name stuff after this story. I Googled "Noah's ark" just now, and the businesses bearing the name, untold millennia after Genesis, include an animal hospital, a day care center, and an antique store. An antique store named after a worldwide deluge. Amazing.

Amazing, because the actual story in Genesis is more horrible than adorable. It's a wrenching tale of God's divine judgment on the world, an aquatic nightmare that wipes away human beings, animals, and property. It's a cataclysmic event whose aftermath leaves a family of eight alone to rebuild a dystopian, post-apocalyptic world.

Our cute nursery wall art and baby books notwithstanding, the story of Noah is a sordid story of human depravity and divine response whose central truths a modern world would just as soon not entertain. Which is why we have done a lot to either sanitize the story or wish it away as a frivolous myth only naïve Sunday school folks believe.

But those of us who take the Bible seriously and really believe in a supernatural God of both judgment and grace have to wrestle with the flood and with the figure at the center—Noah—whose courage and obedience set him apart as one of history's most righteous men. Centuries later, the apostle Peter, who himself knew the terror of the sea, read the account of Noah in Genesis and lauded Noah as a "preacher of righteousness" (2 Peter 2:5). And the writer of Hebrews singled out the patriarch as someone with a fervent faith in the unseen (Heb. 11:7). Jesus referred to "the days of Noah" (Matt. 24), not as a childish fable, but as a real moment in history, as if this universal flood really happened. So there is no reason we shouldn't believe it either, unless, of course, we know more than Jesus and Peter and the writer of Hebrews. I think it's important for Christians to take the Bible at face value and believe that the flood was universal, was supernatural—God caused this flood—and that it isn't a fable or a myth. In fact, most cultures around the world have some version of this story in their ancient histories.

Born just a few generations past Eden, Noah entered the world during a time of rapidly increasing violence, depravity, and sexual perversion. You can just hear the pain and longing in the heart of Noah's father, Lamech. Lamech looked down at his baby boy and prayed that he might be the fulfillment of God's promise of redemption: "Lamech was 182 years old when he fathered a son. And he named him Noah, saying, 'This one will bring us relief from the agonizing labor of our hands, caused by the ground the LORD has cursed'" (Gen. 5:28–29).

Noah's name means *relief* and *rest*. His father, part of the dwindling remnant who still worshiped God, who belonged to a line of believers stretching back to Seth, wished to see the world healed of evil and Eden's curse reversed. What Lamech wouldn't know is that his son would not be the redeemer and his era would not spell rest, but he would be God's chosen vessel through which He rescues humanity. In Noah's day, sin would marble even more deeply into the human heart, inviting a devastating response by God.

In a way, Noah and his family would serve as a sign that God had not given up on humanity, that the fragile seed of the women promised in Genesis 3:15 would yet endure. He would be the only one in his day to stand up against evil. He would be a pariah, his message mocked and ignored. He would be an imperfect shadow of a future son of Lamech, son of Seth, son of Adam, whose triumph over the serpent would usher in God's final rest.

"How is there a cessation from the labors and sorrows in the times of Noah?" asked Origen in the second century. "Jesus only has given rest to humanity and has freed the earth from the curse with which the Lord God cursed it."[2]

✦ The Loneliest Man in the World ✦

August Landmesser is popular on the internet, nearly eight decades after his death. Landmesser is the resister refusing to salute Hitler, surrounded by a throng of compliant German troops, depicted in a viral internet meme. It's an image that has come to exemplify courage. "Be this person," folks will say after posting. Landmesser, who refused to renounce his marriage to a Jewish woman and was therefore drafted into penal military service, was killed in action.

Today we fancy ourselves modern-day August Landmessers, nestled all comfortably in our favorite coffee shop, situated behind our devices. Pressing "send" on that Instagram meme, firing off that well-crafted tweet, forwarding that sharply worded email, we call ourselves brave. But Noah's is a story of *real* courage.

When the world was going one way, Noah dared to be different. Listen again to the way Peter describes him. Noah, the apostle writes, was "a preacher of righteousness, and seven others" (2 Peter 2:5). And "In it a few—that is, eight people—were saved through water" (1 Peter 3:20).

✦ **"A Rage of Bitter Anguish"** ✦

You read that right. Noah preached righteousness and was one of only eight people in the entire world who resisted evil and believed God. The few, the proud, the eight among thousands.

And Noah lived in a world that had gone maddeningly crazy, a downward descent into depravity. This courage wasn't Noah saying no to a second brownie or stopping the Netflix binge at half a season:

> *When the LORD saw that human wickedness was widespread on the earth and that every inclination of the human mind was nothing but evil all the time, the LORD regretted that he had made man on the earth, and he was deeply grieved. Then the LORD said, "I will wipe mankind, whom I created, off the face of the earth, together with the animals, creatures that crawl, and birds of the sky—for*

*I regret that I made them." Noah, however, found favor with
the LORD. (Gen. 6:5–8)*

Genesis doesn't spare language here. *Widespread human wickedness. Every inclination of the human mind. Nothing but evil all the time.*

Every inclination of the heart. And not part of the time. Not some
of the time. All the time. Wickedness and injustice and sensuality so
pronounced and so pervasive, that God reaches for words and language
to give us a window into the way this troubled His heart. We see God
"deeply grieved" and expressing "regret." The language used here is the
strongest and most intense form of human emotion.[3] One scholar calls
it a "rage of bitter anguish."[4]

The world, Genesis tells us, was "filled with violence." Humans,
instead of being fruitful, multiplying, and filling the earth with God's
glory, were filling it with violence. Scholar Gordon Wenham says that
this word violence refers to a "cold-blooded and unscrupulous in-
fringement of the personal rights of others, motivated by greed and
hate and often making use of physical violence and brutality."[5]

The violence, the depravity, the idolatry shattered the heart of
God. The word sometimes translated as "regret" does not denote God
beating Himself up over a mistake—we know from other Scriptures
that God makes no mistakes and is not surprised by anything—but
this is God expressing emotion over human sin.

The present wickedness is set in stark contrast with the simple
faithfulness of Noah. He resisted the spirit of the age. "Noah, however,
found favor with the LORD."

Noah is a fulfillment of God's promise in the garden: that the seed
of the woman and the seed of the serpent would clash. His life is a hint
of final cosmic reversal of the curse, delivered through the offspring of

Eve. Noah's finding favor, Noah's courage and obedience, was God's way of saving humanity and starting over.

✦ Faith, One Nail at a Time ✦

It's hard for us to imagine the sheer difficulty of Noah's life. The entire world, everyone, was going one way and Noah the other. This is easy to do on paper, in the comfort of our very air-conditioned American lives, but Noah was willing to resist his friends, his neighbors, and an entire world system set against God.

Can you imagine how crazy Noah must have seemed to his contemporaries? They lived in a world that had likely never seen a major thunderstorm, much less a worldwide deluge, a flood that would swallow up everything. And yet here he is, not only preaching this message of God's future judgment to those who wouldn't believe it, he's building a massive, mysterious boat. Chuck Swindoll helpfully summarizes just how crazy an undertaking this is for Noah:

- ✦ When Noah started building the ark, his sons weren't even born yet.
- ✦ Noah lived five hundred miles away from the nearest large body of water.
- ✦ The ark's holding capacity was equal to eight modern-day freight trains of sixty-six cars each.[6]

Noah preached this message and built this boat for over a hundred years, ignoring the taunts and the mockery, obeying God nail after nail. I love how the writer of Hebrews describes his courage:

By faith Noah, after he was warned about what was not yet seen and motivated by godly fear, built an ark to deliver his family. By faith he condemned the world and became an heir of the righteousness that comes by faith. (Heb. 11:7)

By faith. By faith. Noah, warned by what was "not seen" and motivated by "godly fear." Noah feared more what he couldn't see—God—than what he could see—his circumstances. This is the essence of faith. Henry Morris accurately describes Noah's faith: "He was moved with fear, not for his own life, but lest his own household be engulfed in the wickedness and ungodliness of the condemned world of his day."[7]

> It's hard for us to imagine the sheer difficulty of Noah's life.

This kind of faith is hard and fragile. Don't think for a moment that Noah didn't have days, maybe weeks or even years, where it all seemed futile. He preached and warned and built for a hundred years while the world around him continued to deteriorate. There was no visible fruit, no sign for him that this was all going to work out, except for the continual presence of God's voice.

Noah's family was with him—his wife, his three sons and their wives, but where was everyone else? And could it be that Noah had other sons and daughters—he was five hundred years old when he began building the ark—who disbelieved, who wrote off their father as crazy, who maybe tuned out his message of repentance and turning toward God? I mean, can you imagine the conversations at home? The first night that Noah comes home and tries to explain this vision he had from God? Did Mrs. Noah think he'd lost it?

I think it's easy to read Genesis and think we'd be right where Noah was. That's how we read history. We are always the good guys in the story. And maybe we'd have the courage to follow God into this for a while. But what about in year fifty when you've got a half-finished boat and still no converts? What about when all his neighbors are mocking him and his friends have all peeled away? Or when the whispers about Noah began circulating at dinner parties. *I used to know him. Something has happened to him. He's gone off the deep end.*

Yet Genesis emphasizes four times that Noah did everything just as God had commanded (Gen. 6:22; 7:5, 9, 16). Not partially, not some, not mostly. Everything. This was a big "everything" to obey. I'm sure he had moments he wondered if he'd gotten it wrong, if the voice he was hearing was something different than God, or, maybe, if perhaps God was wrong. But then he got up the next day and chipped away at the mission.

We tend to think of Noah's ark as big—and it was. Scholars disagree, but generally believe it was around 500 feet long and 50 feet high. It was 1.5 million cubic feet, the equivalent of 250 single-deck railroad cars.[8] Yet it wasn't built quickly. It's not like Noah had power tools and cranes. So he and his sons had to build it slowly, board by board and nail by nail and window by window. Day by day, year by year.

> Genesis emphasizes three times that Noah did everything just as God had commanded. Not partially, not some, not mostly. Everything.

Noah's was not an easy obedience, but the life of faith never is. The single mom who brings her children to church, raising them one verse, one car ride, one dinner at a time. The church planter who builds a movement, one conversation at a time. The doctor who tends to terminal cancer patients, one treatment, one surgery, one grieving family at a time.

We look at the big boat, but the way Noah trusted God was by picking up his hammer every morning and hammering in another nail. By engaging in conversations that warned his neighbors of coming judgment and opportunity for grace. By resisting the spirit of the age.

Noah could live this way because he feared the eternal judgment of God rather than the temporary judgment of his peers. His heart was tuned toward what he could not see, toward the invisible God who ordered his steps. In doing so, Noah joined himself to a long line of the faithful. Generations before, Abel sought the approval of the Lord rather than the safety of his own life. Generations later, Abraham left his home and his family to go to a place he didn't know, following a God he couldn't see. Still later, Joseph believed a God who allowed him to be sold by his brothers and be wrongly convicted of a heinous crime. Daniel prayed to God and was willing to face slaughter by lions. The apostles would face Nero's sword. The early church would rather burn at the stake than deny Christ. And today, martyrs around the world, even as you read this page, are demonstrating the courage to meet in closets and caves, to be imprisoned and sometimes beheaded for their faith. This kind of courage is the hallmark of God's people throughout the ages.

It also flies in the face of so much popular theology. Noah would not see "his best life now." As the writer of Hebrews declares, he believed in what he couldn't see. No converts. No crowds. Just a faithful man obeying God in obscurity.

Today we might mistake Noah for a failure. We'd pull him off the mission field. We'd defund his church plant. We'd put mocking headlines in Christian publications, poking fun at his eccentricity. Noah's life, we'd whisper, seems wasted.

Heaven saw Noah. Heaven sees what we don't see. The boring

steadfastness that seems so out of step, the ordinary Christians without book deals or podcasts or fancy titles who say yes to God in a million small ways every day. The willingness to be different than the world for the sake of the world.

This is different, of course, than a feeling of "persecution" that arises from our own inability to love and live according to the way of Jesus. This is Noah heeding the hard and difficult call, faithfully, steadily, wisely. This is Noah understanding what Jesus would say later, that the way of God is often the lonely and narrow path.

> *If the world hates you, keep in mind that it hated me first. If you belonged to the world, it would love you as its own. As it is, you do not belong to the world, but I have chosen you out of the world. That is why the world hates you. (John 15:18–19 NIV)*

Seems we need periodic reminders of this, of Jesus' call to be willing to resist the winds of culture, to resist the wicked pull of the age, to follow Jesus into the unseen and unknown. D. Martyn Lloyd-Jones said it so well: "What I cannot understand is a person who claims all that is meant by being a Christian and who, at the same time, is afraid of being too good or too holy. That is a contradiction in terms—it is muddled thinking and is indeed a significant confession . . . the fact is that a true Christian, because of what he is, must of necessity stand out in society." Jones says that every follower of Jesus "must so grasp our faith and be properly grasped by it, that if we ever are confronted by such a choice, we shall gladly die for His Name's sake and consider it a supreme honor to lay down our lives for One who laid down His life for us."[9]

Most of us reading that statement won't ever have to face what the apostles faced, what the martyrs throughout history faced, what Noah faced. And yet we meet, every day, the subtle and growing temptation to sand off the rough edges of Christ's Lordship.

The writer of Hebrews says that Noah's faith actually "condemned the world"—an obedience to God so rare, so unique, so different that he stood out. Albert Mohler says it this way: "Whenever an individual lives in obedience to God against the immorality of the world, that individual condemns the rest of the world in its unrighteousness . . . the light stands out from the darkness and what had previously been unseen is revealed for what it truly is."[10]

Jesus would urge His followers to be this kind of light. Resist the temptation to hide the light of our witness "under a bushel" (Matt. 5:15 KJV).

✦ **Grace in the Eyes of the Lord** ✦

There's a line in the King James Version I love. The Bible I memorized as a child says, "Noah found grace in the eyes of the Lord." Other versions translate this phrase from Genesis 6:8 differently, such as "found favor," but I've never gotten over the elegant King James. A world was going downhill fast . . . but there is one man, Noah, who found grace in the eyes of the Lord.

Genesis 6 has faint echoes of Ephesians 2, where Paul writes of the depravity of the godless human heart and then, in words that have echoed across church history, from cathedrals to catacombs to caves, words that have transformed convicts into Christians, sinners into saints.

"But God, who is rich in mercy . . . you are saved by grace."

"But Noah found grace in the eyes of the Lord."

This is the story of Noah. This is the story of the poorest soul who has had an encounter with God. Noah is a man with courage worth emulating, but before Noah had the courage to stand against the mob, to tinker away at a boat nobody would board but his family, he *found grace.* More importantly, grace found Noah.

Genesis is unsparing in its assessment of Noah's character: blameless, righteous, friend of God. But those were the fruits of a man who first found grace.

Finding grace, like Noah, like Paul, has *always* been the message of the Bible. The writer of Hebrews declares, "By faith Noah . . . became an heir of the righteousness that comes by faith" (Heb. 11:7). This was a faith that looked toward the future promise of a redeemer, a promise so far off in the distance, Noah could hardly make out the details. It's the same kind of faith that we, on this side of salvation history, find by gazing backward at Calvary. We behold Jesus and believe with faith that He is the One whom God promised in Eden, of whom the prophets wrote and for whom the people of God longed.

We find grace, and grace finds us.

Undoubtedly, Noah grew up hearing about God from his faithful father, Lamech, who passed down to him the prophetic words of his great-grandfather, Enoch. And yet Noah still had to *find grace* with God. Before Noah was rescued in the ark, Noah was rescued by God and his genuine faith was demonstrated in the way he lived his life.

The Bible describes Noah with three characteristics: he was righteous, he was blameless, and he walked with God. Noah's righteousness set him apart from a wicked world. This is what we might say today about someone when we say, *He's a good man.* He resisted the evil of his day. His blamelessness is something rarely used in the Bible to describe someone. It's a sense of integrity and uprightness. It's a word often used to describe the requirements for animal sacrifices, which were to include animals without blemish.[11] There was nothing anyone could pin on Noah's character. Last, Noah was said to "walk with God." He was not just outwardly righteous and inwardly pure. Noah also cultivated a walk with God. This was also said of his great-grandfather Enoch. He *knew* God.

These are fruits of someone who *found grace* in the eyes of the Lord. This is the fruit of genuine repentance. In Noah's day, a walk with God was cultivated through participating in the animal sacrifices that foreshadowed the day when the final sacrifice, Jesus, would forever atone for the sins of fallen sinners. Today we can walk with God, through repentance and faith, and can come boldly before God's throne. And how do we know we've got grace? Our lives will look like Noah's: growing in righteousness, blamelessness, and walking with God.

Noah didn't perfectly embody blamelessness and neither do we, this side of heaven. Only one could perfectly embody these traits:

- ✦ Only Jesus Christ is perfectly righteous. "Jesus Christ the righteous" (1 John 2:1).
- ✦ Only Jesus Christ is perfectly blameless. "I find no grounds for charging him" (John 19:4).
- ✦ Only Jesus fully walks with God because He is God. "I and the Father are one" (John 10:30).

We can begin the journey toward righteousness, toward blamelessness, because we can walk with God by faith in Christ and by dependence on the Spirit of God who gradually transforms us from children of darkness to children of light, from sons and daughters of Cain to sons and daughters of the King.

◆ **When I Pass Through the Waters** ◆

The Bible doesn't give us a window into Noah's psyche on that boat as it lumbered across the waters. I wonder what those climactic moments were like as God shut the door the final time, and the entreaties toward grace, the hundred years of warning people of judgment, were finally passed. I wonder how Noah managed all of this—his family, the waiting for the floodwaters to recede, the animals, the long days and hard nights clinging to God's promise to deliver them. I wonder how Noah felt at the first signs of water receding, when the final dove was sent out and didn't come back, the signal that they could step off the boat after 370 long days and nights—150 days of the flood, 150 more days while the waters recede, another 70 days for the earth to dry.[12] How did they change after a year of their lives they'd never forget, now entering a world empty of people and life but exploding with creative possibility?

And yet the story of Noah is larger than his single life. There is rich symbolism that points us forward, that locates the flood and the ark in the greater narrative of redemption and salvation in Scripture.

First, this story is a symbol both of God's judgment and of God's grace. The apostle Peter, in warning his God's judgment, writes, "if [God] didn't spare the ancient world, but protected Noah, a preacher of righteousness, and seven others, when he brought the flood on the world of the ungodly" (2 Peter 2:5). Peter's word to the people of his day and to our present day is that God has not changed, humans have sinned against Him, and that there is certain judgment coming. This is a hard message for modern people to hear, quite frankly, and one that we pastors are often uncomfortable preaching. How can a good God send a worldwide flood that would send people to their deaths? How can a good God send people to hell?

And yet the ark is also a picture of salvation. Peter elsewhere describes God's character, saying that He "patiently waited" (1 Peter 3:20). Noah preached salvation for one hundred years, day after day, to people who refused to listen, who refused to hear that something terrible was coming. The tragic story of Noah's ark is that it was built for more than eight people. More could have been spared God's judgment, if they'd only listened and believed Noah.

Jesus compared the apathy of Noah's day to the response of people in this age:

> But concerning that day and hour no one knows, not even the angels of heaven, nor the Son, but the Father only. For as were the days of Noah, so will be the coming of the Son of Man. For as in those days before the flood they were eating and drinking, marrying and giving in marriage, until the day when Noah entered the ark, and they were unaware until the flood came and swept them all away, so will be the coming of the Son of Man. (Matt. 24:36–39 ESV)

God is warning the world—through His Word, through faithful messengers—that there is certain judgment coming. This is an uncomfortable truth. None of us wants to be seen as a "fire and brimstone" preacher. And while there are many Christians who seem to weirdly revel in the punishment of the wicked, the Bible is sober about the reality of human beings. We have sinned against God. We deserve the sure judgment coming. And yet God is patient. So patient He sent warning after warning to the people of Noah's day and is sending warnings today that there is a way of escape

> The tragic story of Noah's ark is that it was built for more than eight people.

through faith in God's own Son, Jesus. The same God who called Noah and provided the ark as a way of escape is the same God who sent Jesus as a way of escape from hell. "The wages of sin," Romans tells us, "is death, but the gift of God is eternal life through Jesus Christ our Lord" (Rom. 6:23). We should not see the God of the Old Testament as a capricious deity who delights in striking down people, but as a patient, longsuffering God who, as the Bible says is "not wanting any to perish but all to come to repentance" (2 Peter 3:9).

In this the ark is a picture of salvation. As Noah and his family climbed aboard the ark and received salvation, so those who put their faith in Jesus cling to the cross and receive salvation. As God shuts the door, He secures us and preserves us. Noah and his family, ultimately, were not saved by their own moral goodness, but by their faith that God would save them and so it is that we are saved not by our own moral goodness, but by faith in Christ who saves us.

Albert Mohler says it this way, "The ark and those who stand in it are a picture of the church. Noah is the exemplar who exercises faith and is saved from God's watery judgment." He continues, "Even in the midst of the Old Testament's most horrific display of God's wrath, we find an extraordinary display of the grace of God."[13]

And Bruce Waltke says the ark "gives evidence that the sovereign, merciful Lord preserves a righteous remnant of covenant people during the darkest crises of their history. Although the whole corrupt world perishes in the flood, God preserves for himself one family."[14] This is a theme throughout Scripture. God preserved a remnant of Israel through times of apostasy and even as they scattered into exile and on into their return to their homeland. He has promised to preserve His new creation people in the church (Matt. 16:17–19). Nothing, Paul tells us in Romans, can separate God's people from His love (Rom. 8:38–39). Nothing, Jesus tells us in John, can pluck us out of the Father and the Son's hand (John 10:28–30).

We are the people who passed through the waters of God's judgment. Peter says that our baptism—this symbol of dying with Christ and rising again in new life, is a sign that we have a "good conscience" toward God (1 Peter 3:21). God rescuing His people from the waters is a recurring symbol of grace throughout Scripture. Sandra Richter writes:

> Throughout the story there is a recurring theme of Yahweh rescuing his people by delivering them from the sea. First there is creation, in which God contains and directs the sea such that its great power is harnessed to serve the needs of the created order. Then there is the flood, in which God makes uses of the ark to rescue his people from the sea and therefore from judgment. Then the great deliverance under Moses in which God parts the Red Sea such that his people pass through on dry ground. Next Joshua leads the children of Abraham into the Promised Land by parting the Jordan River—and again God's people pass through safely on dry ground. And then there is this young rabbi from Nazareth who finds himself on the Sea of Galilee on a stormy day . . . the young Nazarene, seeing the fear in the eyes of his friends, stands up and speaks to the sea. And the sea, as it had on the morning of creation, obeys him.[15]

The story of Noah ultimately tells us of a God who rescues His people from the waters of judgment. This is why we can read Noah's story and see in it God's promise "when you pass through the waters, I will be with you" (Isa. 43:2). We've seen Jesus pass through the waters for us, approved by God as the Spirit descended like the dove in Noah's day, signaling the way to peace with God. We can know the God who declares to us, in Jesus, "If anyone thirsts, let him come to me and drink," and says, "The one who believes in me, as the Scripture has said, will have streams of living water flow from deep within him" (John 7:38), and who is leading us to that new final home, where we are promised a "new heaven and new earth" and "where there is no sea." No more sea means no more waters of judgment. It means that in Christ there is therefore no condemnation.

This is the story of Noah. In one sense, it's a story about a courageous man who stood against the culture of his day, faithfully obeying God. In another sense, Noah points us toward someone greater who rescues His people from the water. Noah may have lived a life characterized by blamelessness and righteousness, but he didn't walk with God perfectly. We know this because at the end of his life, after the flood, we see an image of Noah passed out drunk and naked, having indulged his worst impulses. It's a shocking scene, one that we'd wish Moses had left on the cutting-room floor as he wrote Genesis. But God didn't allow Noah's biography to be airbrushed, tidied up so that we could only see the noble parts. Noah was a sinner in need of God's saving grace—just like the rest of us.

CHAPTER NINE

The Descendants

Shem, Ham, Japheth, and God's New Creation

The last man on earth is not alone" reads the haunting description of *I Am Legend*, the 2007 post-apocalyptic thriller starring Will Smith as a virologist who survives a lethal outbreak that either kills humans or turns them into violent monsters. The scenes are haunting as Smith roams the hollowed-out streets of New York City, looking for signs of life.

This doesn't do justice, really, to the landscape that the family of Noah found as they finally exited the ark after a year in which the world was destroyed while they floated among the ruins. Legs wobbly, eyes adjusting to the sunlight, their breath coming in shocked gasps as the world they had left—teeming with life and humanity, with art, architecture, and music, with vegetation and livestock—had given way to barrenness. As the floodwaters receded, the survivors beheld a wasteland.

This was a world they would be tasked to rebuild. Imagine this monumental assignment. Rebuilding a city is *hard*. After Katrina devastated the United States Gulf Coast, it took years and tears and money, and still there are some areas yet to be restored to their pre-hurricane glory. Rebuilding involves digging out. It involves tearing down. It involves drawing new property lines and imagining new neighbor-hoods where nature swept away the old.

The task before Noah's family was not just rebuilding a city but re-building the world. And yet Genesis reminds us that this is not merely a human project. "God remembered Noah" (Gen. 8:1). It was not that God had forgotten Noah, sealed off with his family and the animals in their seagoing wooden prison. No, "God remembered Noah" means that God "acts according to His covenant promises, especially in a way evident to His people."[1] It means that while one world had faded away, another was emerging, that while God was destroying, He was also restoring, building, creating something new. It means God saw that family that stepped off the ark that day. And that family also, after 370 hard and difficult days, remembered God:

> *Then Noah built an altar to the LORD. He took some of every kind of clean animal and every kind of clean bird and offered burnt offerings on the altar. When the LORD smelled the pleasing aroma, he said to himself, "I will never again curse the ground because of human beings, even though the inclination of the human heart is evil from youth onward. And I will never again strike down every living thing as I have done.*
>
> *As long as the earth endures,*
> *seedtime and harvest, cold and heat,*
> *summer and winter, and day and night*
> *will not cease." (Gen. 8:20–22)*

The world, God's world, the one He had declared "good" at the first breaths of creation, would continue. The flood was, to quote Old Testament scholar Sandra Richter, a work of "decreation" that would now give way to the work of re-creation: "What we see in the flood is not merely a natural disaster intended to bring about God's judgment on humanity, but a *de-creational* event. What had been done at creation is undone with the flood. The world is brought back to its pre-creation state—formless and void."[2]

✦ **After the Deluge: The Promise** ✦

And yet we read in Genesis that "God remembered Noah" (Gen. 8:1). I love this phrase, repeated often in the Old Testament. When God "remembers" we should not think of it as God recalling who Noah and his family were. God is omniscient; He knows everything. God doesn't forget people. But God's "remember" is deeper. It implies that God saw Noah and that God would act on behalf of Noah.

I imagine Noah and his family would have felt forgotten, bobbing up and down in that old boat. Wouldn't you? I imagine his sons and their wives wondering, asking, hoping for what was next. Have you ever been in a season like this in your life, where God allowed a great disruption in your world and you find yourself clinging to some sign, some clue, some pathway for what might be ahead of you? I have been in those hard seasons myself. I'm in one of those seasons right now. There is both remorse and sadness about what you have left behind and a bit of thrill of what might be next.

Which is why it is important to see that the first act of Noah's family when leaving the ark was to worship the God who saved them. God remembered Noah but Noah remembered God. Noah offered the best of his livestock, sacrificing animals as an act of costly worship. Noah, saved by God's hand from God's own judgment of the world, would perform a sacrifice in the death of an innocent animal that points forward to the day when Jesus—God's innocent Lamb—would be sacrificed to save His people from coming judgment.

God's response was not only to accept this sacrifice, much as He would accept Abel's sacrifice, much as He would accept the sacrifice of the Son on Calvary, He also issued a new covenant with the family of Noah:

> *"Understand that I am establishing my covenant with you and your descendants after you, and with every living creature that is with you—birds, livestock, and all wildlife of the earth that are with you— all the animals of the earth that came out of the ark. I establish my covenant with you that never again will every creature be wiped out by floodwaters; there will never again be a flood to destroy the earth."*
>
> *And God said, "This is the sign of the covenant I am making between me and you and every living creature with you, a covenant for all future generations: I have placed my bow in the clouds, and it will be a sign of the covenant between me and the earth. Whenever I form clouds over the earth and the bow appears in the clouds, I will remember my covenant between me and you and all the living creatures: water will never again become a flood to destroy every creature. The bow will be in the clouds, and I will look at it and remember the permanent covenant between God and all the living creatures on earth." God said to Noah, "This is the sign of the covenant that I have established between me and every creature on earth." (Gen. 9:9–17)*

This covenant is a promise not dependent on human behavior, but God's declaration that He would never again destroy the earth with a flood. To signify His promise, God pointed to the rainbow in the sky and declared this would remind humans of His faithfulness. There is significance here in the language Moses uses to describe God's guarantee to Noah's family. The Hebrew words for rainbow are warrior language. David Atkinson writes movingly about this sign: "The hostility is over: God hangs up his bow! The covenant is nothing man-made. In its spectral beauty, it tells us only of the Creator—and that the light of his beauty shines through even the reminders of his watery judgment. The weapon of war itself is transformed into a delight. Here is the Creator's overarching care: the Creator God is the Covenant God. He who made us still loves us."[3]

He who made us still loves us. This rainbow is God's sign that He had not given up on humanity. God is for humanity. This is what we see every single time we view a rainbow after a rainstorm. We can look to the heavens, from wherever we live on this planet, and behold and see God's faithfulness. God, who formed humans from the dust of the ground and breathed into humans the breath of life, who sent His Son to the earth in human flesh, loves human souls and human bodies. The rainbow reminds us of the words of the writer of Hebrews who declares that the Godhead is "sustaining all things by his powerful word" (Heb. 1:3). Wiersbe sees in the rainbow a sign of God's promise of redemption in Jesus: "But He has turned the bow toward heaven and taken the punishment for us Himself!"[4]

You will notice that God didn't merely make a covenant with humanity, but with the entire cosmos. This demonstrates God's care for the earth. The Bible tells us that Creation is a testimony, a signpost to the Creator:

The heavens declare the glory of God,
and the expanse proclaims the work of his hands.
Day after day they pour out speech;
night after night they communicate knowledge.
There is no speech; there are no words;
their voice is not heard.
Their message has gone out to the whole earth,
and their words to the ends of the world. (Ps. 19:1–4)

This is why when the family of Noah stepped off that boat and into a devastated new world, God's instructions were similar to His instructions to their ancestor, Adam, centuries earlier. God had not given up on His creation and was once again tasking His image-bearers to do the work of cultivating and creating, of building and multiplying. "God said to Noah, 'As for you, be fruitful and increase in number; multiply upon the earth . . .'" (Gen. 9:7 NIV).

✦ Into a Different World ✦

And yet as much as the family of Noah was assuming the role of a new Adam, their mandate would be fulfilled in a world so much different than Eden. Noah's sons would go out into a world not pure and innocent, fresh and vibrant like Eden, but a world requiring re-creation and renewal, the scars of God's judgment on every uprooted tree and toppled home.

This would be a work of rebuilding conducted under the dark reality of a fallen world, God's hopeful covenant tinged with the boundary markers of a world where sin was still a present reality. Whereas before Adam had dominion over the creation, here now God tells the family of Noah that creation would be taught to fear humans:

> *The fear and terror of you will be in every living creature on the earth, every bird of the sky, every creature that crawls on the ground, and all the fish of the sea. They are placed under your authority. (Gen. 9:2)*

The harmony between humans and creation, destroyed when Eve chose the way of the serpent, would give way to antagonism and fear. The animal kingdom would now see humans as a threat—and in so many ways, humans would be tempted to exploit the creation instead of assume responsibility for its care.

And even in a world just cleansed by judgment, violence among image-bearers would still be a reality, with new rules for human government:

> *I will require a penalty for your lifeblood; I will require it from any animal and from any human; if someone murders a fellow human, I will require that person's life.*
>
> > *Whoever sheds human blood,*
> > *by humans his blood will be shed,*
> > *for God made humans in his image. (Gen. 9:5–6)*

God here is at once reminding Noah of the dignity with which He has endowed human beings. Even in a fallen world, human beings bear the full image of God, a concept that is unique to the Christian story. This marker is important, for in a broken world, in every generation there are violent temptations for powerful humans to prey upon the weak and for elevation of animals to the same level as humanity.

Though God assigned Adam and Eve authority and stewardship

over creation, here God lays out some basic principles for the way humans govern themselves in a fallen world. Most of us have opinions about how government should work, but we can't deny its need. Places where there is anarchy, or a lack of order, descend into chaos and only end in the powerful exploiting the less powerful. This is the theme of the book of Judges, where it is said at the end, "Everyone did whatever seemed right to him" (Judg. 17:6). Three institutions are given by God for human flourishing, two of which we see here in the opening chapters of Genesis: the family and human government. Later God would establish the third institution, the church.

This mandate would mostly fall not on Noah but on Noah's sons, from whom would come the future of humanity. They'd be charged with building their families and doing the work of creation in a hostile world still recovering from catastrophe. And in many ways this is the same reality in which we live, on the one hand heeding God's call to worship Him by obeying the call to lead our families and use our hands and minds to do work that glorifies Him, to create and renew and rebuild. And yet we do this under the dark cloud of sin that is so embedded in the human experience, in a planet both teeming with beauty and life yet groaning under the weight of the fall. We, like Noah's sons, live in the in-between, lamenting the way sin has distorted Eden and yet longing and hopeful for God's full promise of re-creation to arrive in its fullness.

Understanding this reality of re-creation and renewal should shape the way we see the world. It keeps us from both deep cynicism at the brokenness we see around us—the babies aborted, the refugees turned away, the evil that slinks around our cities—and yet should also keep us from the triumphalism that causes us to think we can make a world after Noah completely perfect before Jesus returns in triumph.

God's work here of re-creation and re-newal is a theme throughout the story of sal-vation. Here in Noah's day it is a small sign of the kingdom of God, where Jesus would come and begin His work to reverse the curse, to open blind eyes, to make the lame walk, to turn back the raging sea, and to raise the dead to new life. Isaiah (43:19) declares of God,

> Understanding this reality of re-creation and renewal should shape the way we see the world.

"Look, I am about to do something new," a promise repeated and fulfilled in Revelation (21:5).

This is why Christians can rejoice amidst all that seems so wrong in the world. We see that God is working to renew and restore not just a broken planet, but broken people. Paul declares that everyone in Christ "is a new creation; the old has passed away, and see, the new has come!" (2 Cor. 5:17). This is the work God is doing in the world, the work God is doing in the hearts of people.

Like the earth after the flood, human hearts are vast wastelands, void of beauty and awash in the wreckage of sin, but the Spirit of God delights in turning cold and sinful hearts to hearts that burst with joy toward their Creator. The prophet Ezekiel predicted this age would come, that God's spirit would dawn: "I will give you a new heart and put a new spirit within you; I will remove your heart of stone and give you a heart of flesh" (Ezek. 36:26). In a sense, the promise of the rain-bow is the lived reality of those who have been redeemed by Jesus, who absorbed the punishment for sin so that we could be saved aboard the ark of salvation. Now He is re-creating us. We have "have put on the new self. You are being renewed in knowledge according to the image of your Creator" (Col. 3:10).

Every miracle of Jesus in the New Testament is an act of God's re-creation, a pushback against the curse of sin on the earth, a sign of the death of Satan's grip on the world. And every single person who confesses that Jesus is Lord is an act of God's re-creation. "He gave them a covenant, a covenant embellished with a divine symbol and ratified with its own signature written out in all the colors of beauty," writes Charles Spurgeon. "We too stand under a covenant that has its own faithful witness in heaven, more transcendently illustrious and beautiful than the rainbow—the person of Christ Jesus our Lord."[5]

✦ When Good People Do Bad Things ✦

Yet as these righteous men begin the work of re-creation, of filling the earth and subduing it for God's glory, they, like their ancestors, are tempted by the same things that lure humans today. The end of the chronicle of Noah's family includes a story most of us would just as soon stay on the cutting-room floor. And yet it's here in the pages of Scripture, reminding us that even the best, most courageous of God's people is woefully imperfect.

Noah is perhaps one of the most righteous men in all of Scripture, lauded by the prophets, by Jesus, by the writer of Hebrews as an example of unswerving courage and faithfulness in the face of a culture that was opposed to God. He is probably one of the best leaders in human history, on the Mount Rushmore of most admired men. Still, Genesis gives us a window into a story on the back end of Noah's life, a reminder that even the best humans are fallen and there is only one human who was truly righteous enough to save humanity.

And it's sordid. Noah is found in his tent, drunk and naked. Bible scholars are mixed on exactly what this may mean, but at the very least we know that Noah was guilty of the sin of drunkenness and of exposure. Later the prophets would condemn this behavior as wicked: "Woe to him who gives his neighbors drink, pouring out your wrath and even making them drunk, in order to look at their nakedness" (Hab. 2:15).

It's hard to imagine how the man who for a hundred years stood against the world with courage, who faithfully built the ark according to God's commands, who shepherded his family through the flood, was now, at the end of his life, embarrassed and fallen. And it's also hard to imagine how Noah's son Ham, who like the rest of his family obeyed God when it was hard, who was a righteous man saved from God's judgment, finds himself reveling and voyeuristic.

For Noah, you wonder if this was a lackadaisical approach to his spiritual life, years after the high points of his radical obedience and building of the ark. To get drunk means this episode likely happened years after they stepped off the ark. The grapes had to grow and ripen to produce fermented alcohol. And there is mention of his grandchildren. Kent Hughes laments Noah's fall:

> Noah's folly is recorded to make us wise. His pathetic example demonstrates that people in their prime, and even in their old age, are sometimes overtaken by sensualities that they before had avoided. I have known this because it has been told to me for years. But now I can feel it—the tendency to allow myself indulgences that I avoided when younger, be they visual or mental or physical, with the dismissive line that "I'm too old for these things to harm me." The tendency is to ease up when the conflicts lessen. When all the world was against

Noah, he faced scorn and violence straight-up. But in his vineyard among his own who needed no proof of his virtue, he relaxed.[6]

This is a temptation for all of us, to let down our guard, to stop participating with the Spirit of God in the fight against sin. Sadly, in recent years, we've seen good men, whose words and life brought many to salvation in Christ, yield to gross sins in their private lives. The headlines are almost daily and it's sad. We shouldn't look at Noah with self-righteousness, but with pity and with a sober realization that if we think we are beyond these sins, we might be the most vulnerable to their entrance into our lives.

It's also a sober reminder that sometimes good men do bad things or make bad choices. In my decades in ministry, I've seen men I admired make poor choices, choices that hurt me and others. It's hard to witness up close. And perhaps you are reading this as the victim of someone else's poor choices. The only salve I can give a heart hurt by the church is that God included this story of Noah's scandal, in part, so we'd look past the worship of men and fix our gaze on the One who, naked on a cross, bore our shame; who was perfect and lovely and yet took your sins and my sins so we might find peace with God.

✦ Canaan's Curse and Christ's Redemption ✦

Noah's three sons each caught their father in gross behavior, but their reactions are a lesson in the seriousness of sin. Ham was the first to see, but rather than turning his head and covering his father's sin and shame, Ham looked and lingered, the sin of Noah manifesting in even grosser, lustful, sexual sin in his son. Let's not forget that in this moment, Ham is not just a son but a father, a husband, a leader in the community. Not only did he look, he passed on the sordid details, embarrassing his father and refusing to honor the patriarch.

The response by the other two sons, Shem and Japheth, are illustrations of the right approach. They covered their father and walked backward, refusing to indulge further in sin and in an act of grace, covering his sin. What a demonstration of grace. Proverbs 17:9 reminds us that "Whoever conceals an offense promotes love, but whoever gossips about it separates friends." "Love covers a multitude of sins," we are told in 1 Peter 4:8, and "How joyful is the one whose transgression is forgiven, whose sin is covered!" the psalmist writes in Psalm 32.

This is not about hiding sin or covering up corruption, but about resisting the urge to revel in the transgressions of others, a virtual pastime in this digital tabloid age. In a way, Shem and Japheth image Jesus, who doesn't revel in the sins of His people but sacrificed Himself to cover them.

For this, God pronounces a curse, not on Ham, but on Ham's son, Canaan. This can seem a bit of a mystery. Why would the son suffer the punishment for the father's sins? But let's remember that Genesis was written to the people of Israel, whose chief enemy was the Canaanites, a wicked, sensual and bloodthirsty people. Scholar Kenneth Matthews says: "In this case the curse is directed at Ham's son as Ham's just deserts for the disrespect he had toward his own father, Noah. Yet the imprecation was spoken against future generations of Canaanites who would suffer subjugation 'not because of the sins of Ham, but because they themselves acted like Ham, because of their own transgressions.'"[7]

Some have erroneously taught that this curse is a reason for the practice of chattel slavery, as if God had permanently consigned a people to subjugation and dehumanization. This was taught by white slave owners in the antebellum South as a way of spiritually justifying their slave owning. This is based on the false idea that the curse extended to Ham's descendants in perpetuity and that all of Ham's descendants settled in Africa. But not only is this a wicked twisting of Scripture, which teaches the dignity of every human being (Gen. 1:26) and prohibits slavery as sin (Ex. 21:16; 1 Tim. 1:8–10), but descendants of Ham became peoples across the Middle East and around the world. What's more, it seems the curse on Canaan was fulfilled by Israel's conquest of Canaan.[8] Interestingly, as part of Israel's conquest of Jericho, a daughter of Canaan named Rahab would marry into the family of Israel and join God's people in covenant faithfulness.

The sons of Noah, Shem, Ham, and Japheth, are the fathers of the human race, their families becoming the peoples who populate the world. It would be from the line of Shem from whom God's promise of a redeemer would come. God would call from this family a man named Abraham who would be the father of Israel. From Israel would come a family named Judah, and from Judah a family named David, who would be Israel's greatest king.

Jesus, the Son of Adam, the son of Noah, the son of Shem, the son of Abraham, the son of David, would bear His own curse to bring into His new family sons of Ham, sons of Shem, and sons of Japheth. In a beautiful display of the racial reconciliation brought about by Christ's sacrificial death and resurrection, the book of Acts shows us that in God's new family, a son of Ham in the Ethiopian eunuch, a son of Japheth in Cornelius and sons of Shem in Peter and Paul.[9]

God's work of reconciliation and re-creation is the theme of Genesis, a book that both tells us how our story began and also points us forward toward the end of our story. Genesis invites us to see ourselves as God sees us, image-bearers of the Almighty, and yet beckons us to fall on our knees in worship and repentance of the One who has come to make us new.

I pray this book ushers you into seeing your story as part of God's story and to accept the call of Jesus to know the One who formed you with care—from the very beginning.

ACKNOWLEDGMENTS

This is my eleventh published book and I don't take for granted any opportunity God gives me to publish. From the time I was a little kid, I dreamed of being a writer and so many good people have worked hard to make this dream a reality. First, my parents were so encouraging all along the way, telling me one day that I'd be a published author even when it seemed so impossible and daunting. Then in 2002, I married an amazing woman named Angela who has been a faithful friend and support, even putting up with my late nights and early mornings spent hunched over my laptop. I also give a lot of credit to my wonderful children, Grace, Daniel, Emma, and Lily, who encourage me and provide much inspiration for these pages.

I have to also thank my good friend Drew Dyck, who has been a faithful friend all these years, first publishing me when he was at *Christianity Today* and now as editor at Moody, publishing me again and again. I'm thankful to Betsey Newenhuyse, whom I first met when she was editor of *Moody Monthly* and I was sending in really bad article pitches, and she patiently coached me up and is now editing my Moody manuscripts. She's a fantastic editor.

I'm indebted to my agent, Erik Wolgemuth, who has the patience of Job, putting up with my flurry of publishing ideas and helping coach me along this publishing journey.

Last, I want to thank every pastor who has ever preached the book of Genesis and kindled in my heart a love for this most magnificent first book of Scripture. It is my prayer that this book does the same for you readers. After all, it is you readers who allow us writers to do what we do, to have an audience for the words God has put on our hearts.

NOTES

Introduction ◆ In the Beginning, God

1. Bruce K. Waltke, *Genesis: A Commentary* (Grand Rapids, MI: Zondervan Academic, 2016), 56.

2. Derek Kidner, *Genesis: An Introduction and Commentary* (London: Tyndale, 1967), 47.

3. James Montgomery Boice, *Genesis: An Expositional Commentary, Vol. 1: Genesis 1–11* (Grand Rapids, MI: Baker Books, 1998).

4. John M. Frame, *Systematic Theology: An Introduction to Christian Belief* (Phillipsburg, NJ: P & R Publishing, 2013), 363.

5. Kidner, *Genesis*, 51.

6. Frame, *Systematic Theology*, 185.

7. Waltke, *Genesis*, 69.

8. David J. Atkinson, *The Message of Genesis 1–11* (Downers Grove, IL: InterVarsity Press, 2017), 16.

9. Wayne Grudem, *Systematic Theology: An Introduction to Biblical Doctrine* (Grand Rapids, MI: Zondervan, 1994), 268–70.

10. "A Theology of Creation in 12 Points," Desiring God, March 11, 2016, https://www.desiringgod.org/interviews/a-theology-of-creation-in-12-points.

11. A. W. Tozer, *The Knowledge of the Holy* (1961), in *A. W. Tozer: Three Spiritual Classics in One Volume* (Chicago: Moody, 2018), 13.

12. John H. Walton, *The NIV Application Commentary Genesis* (Grand Rapids, MI: Zondervan Academic, 2001), 66.

13. Kenneth Mathews, *The New American Commentary: Genesis 1–11:26* (Nashville, TN: Holman Reference, 1996).

14. Sandra L. Richter, *The Epic of Eden: A Christian Entry into the Old Testament* (Downers Grove, IL: InterVarsity Press, 2010), 128.

15. Ibid., 129.

Chapter 1 ❖ The Delinquent: Adam, First, Fallen, and Forgiven

1. Thomas R. Schreiner, *Paul, Apostle of God's Glory in Christ: A Pauline Theology* (Downers Grove, IL: IVP Academic, 2006), 154.

2. Francis A. Schaeffer, *Genesis in Space and Time: The Flow of Biblical History* (Downers Grove, IL: InterVarsity Press, 1972), 33.

3. Daniel Darling, *The Dignity Revolution: Reclaiming God's Rich Vision for Humanity* (Charlotte, NC: The Good Book Company, 2018), 23–24.

4. James Montgomery Boice, *Genesis, an Expositional Commentary* (Grand Rapids, MI: Zondervan, 1982), 78.

5. Andrew Louth, ed., *Genesis 1–11* (Ancient Commentary on Scripture: Old Testament, Volume 1) (Downers Grove, IL: InterVarsity Press, 2001), 28.

6. To read the best arguments on this, check out *Four Views on The Historical Adam*, edited by Matthew Barrett and Ardel B. Caneday and published in 2013 by Zondervan. I found myself especially resonating with the arguments by John Collins. I also highly recommend the final chapter by Phil Ryken on how a literal Adam is essential to understanding the entire gospel narrative in Scripture. You might also check out Collins's work, *Did Adam and Eve Really Exist?* (Crossway, 2011).

7. Millard J. Erickson, *Christian Theology*, 3rd edition (Grand Rapids, MI: Baker Academic, 2013), 442.

8. Ardel B. Caneday, Matthew Barrett, and Stanley N. Gundry, eds., *Four Views on the Historical Adam* (Grand Rapids, MI: Zondervan Academic, 2013), 268–270.

9. "Sin's Advantage in the Law by R. C. Sproul," Ligonier Ministries, accessed July 9, 2021, https://www.ligonier.org/learn/sermons/sins-advantage-law/.

10. Schreiner, *Paul, Apostle of God's Glory in Christ*, 154.

11. Derek Kidner, *Genesis: An Introduction and Commentary* (London: Tyndale, 1967), 74.

12. David J. Atkinson, *The Message of Genesis 1–11* (Downers Grove, IL: InterVarsity Press, 2017), 33–34.

13. Charles Wesley, 1739, altered by Martin Madan, 1760, in *The Service of Song for Baptist Churches* (New York: Sheldon and Company, 1876), 97.

Chapter 2 ❖ The Forbidden: Eve, the Misled Mother of All

1. Umberto Cassuto, *From Adam to Noah: A Commentary on the Book of Genesis I-VI* (Jerusalem: The Hebrew University Magnes Press, 1961), 134.

2. "The Politics of Loneliness Is Totalitarian," *The Week*, accessed July 16, 2021, https://theweek.com/politics/1002095/the-politics-of-loneliness-is-totalitarian.

3. There are two great resources on this: Curt Thomson's work in *The Soul of Shame* and *The Anatomy of the Soul* are really good, along with the work of sociologist Jean Twenge whose book *iGen* on the effects of digital communication on young brains is really insightful.

4. Matthew Henry and J. B. Williams, *Exposition of the Old and New Testament* (James Nisbet, 1828), 13.

5. *Genesis*, Calvin's Commentaries, vol. 1, trans. and rev. by John King (Grand Rapids, MI: Baker Academic, 1999), 133.

6. *The Poetical Works of Milton, Young, Gray, Beattie, and Collins* (J. Grigg, 1831), 70.

7. Mary Kassian, "Complementarianism for Dummies," The Gospel Coalition, accessed July 17, 2021, https://www.thegospelcoalition.org/article/complementarianism-for-dummies/.

8. Derek Kidner, *Genesis: An Introduction and Commentary* (London: Tyndale, 1967), 70.

9. Sandra L. Richter, *The Epic of Eden: A Christian Entry into the Old Testament* (Downers Grove, IL: InterVarsity Press, 2010), 104.

10. Ibid., 92.

11. Michael F. Bird, *Evangelical Theology: A Biblical and Systematic Introduction* (Grand Rapids, MI: Zondervan, 2013), 498.

12. Kidner, *Genesis*, 73.

13. Amy Gannett, "3 Ways Complementarian Pastors Can Encourage Women," The Gospel Coalition, accessed July 17, 2021, https://www.thegospelcoalition.org/article/3-ways-complementarian-pastors-can-encourage-women/.

14. "The Truth about Pain in Childbearing," Jen Wilkin, accessed July 19, 2021, https://www.jenwilkin.net/blog/2011/08/truth-about-pain-in-childbearing.html.

Chapter 3 ✦ The Deceiver: Satan, Fallen from Glory, Father of Lies

1. Tony Evans, *The Truth about Angels and Demons* (Chicago: Moody, 2005), 61.

2. John H. Walton, *The NIV Application Commentary Genesis* (Grand Rapids, MI: Zondervan Academic, 2001), 123.

3. David J. Atkinson, *The Message of Genesis 1–11* (Downers Grove, IL: InterVarsity Press, 2017), 81.

4. "Spiritual Beings," The Bible Project, accessed July 20, 2021, https://d1bsmz3sdi-hplr.cloudfront.net/media/Study%20Notes/SBS_00_Series_VN_final_updated.pdf. See also, Michael S. Heiser, *Demons: What the Bible Really Says about the Powers of Darkness* (Bellingham, WA: Lexham Press, 2020).

5. Darrell Bock, *Luke* (Baker Exegetical Commentary on the New Testament) (Grand Rapids, MI: Baker Academic, 1996), 1006.

6. James Montgomery Boice, *Genesis, an Expositional Commentary* (Grand Rapids, MI: Zondervan, 1982), 153.

7. C. John Collins, *Genesis 1–4: A Linguistic, Literary, and Theological Commentary* (P&R Publishing, Phillipsburg, NJ: 2006), 171.

8. Bruce K. Waltke, *Genesis: A Commentary* (Grand Rapids, MI: Zondervan Academic, 2016), 91.

9. Atkinson, *The Message of Genesis 1–11*, 82.

10. Derek Kidner, *Genesis: An Introduction and Commentary* (London: Tyndale, 1967), 72.

11. Waltke, *Genesis*, 92.

12. Ibid., 92.

13. Russell Moore, *Tempted and Tried: Temptation and the Triumph of Christ* (Wheaton, IL: Crossway, 2011), 36–37.

14. Heiser, *Demons*, 192–93.

15. Martin Luther, "A Mighty Fortress," trans. Frederic Henry Hedge, in *Psalms and Hymns, and Spiritual Songs: Manual of Worship for the Church of Christ*, comp. and ed. Charles S. Robinson (New York: A. S. Barnes and Company, 1876), 165.

Chapter 4 ✦ The Slain Sacrifice: Abel and the Cost of Discipleship

1. Warren W. Wiersbe, *Be Confident (Hebrews): Live by Faith Not by Sight* (The BE Series Commentary) (Colorado Springs, CO: David C. Cook, 1982), 167.

2. "Boko Haram Kill Villagers in Christmas Eve Attack," *BBC News*, December 25, 2020, sec. Africa, https://www.bbc.com/news/world-africa-55448105.

3. PastorAppreciation1, *2021 Day of the Christian Martyr*, accessed July 22, 2021, https://www.youtube.com/watch?v=x2zHWM1R378.

4. Todd Nettleton and The Voice of the Martyrs, *When Faith Is Forbidden: 40 Days on the Frontlines with Persecuted Christians* (Chicago: Moody, 2021), 75–77.

5. Robert Alter, *The Five Books of Moses: A Translation with Commentary* (New York: W. W. Norton & Company, 2008), 29.

6. Bruce K. Waltke, *Genesis: A Commentary* (Grand Rapids, MI: Zondervan Academic, 2016), 97.

7. Kenneth Matthews, *The New American Commentary: Genesis 1–11:26* (Nashville, TN: Holman Reference, 1996), 269.

8. *Luther's Works*, vol. 1, Jaroslav Jan Pelikan, gen. ed. (St. Louis: Concordia Publishing House, 1958), 251.

9. George H. Guthrie, *NIV Application Commentary: Hebrews* (Grand Rapids, MI: Zondervan Academic, 1998), 422.

Chapter 5 ✦ The Marked: Cain and the Price of Self-Worship

1. Warren W. Wiersbe, *The Wiersbe Bible Commentary: New Testament* (Colorado Springs: David C Cook, 2003), 121.

2. Robert Alter, *The Five Books of Moses: A Translation with Commentary* (New York: W. W. Norton & Company, 2008), 29.

3. Hebrew scholar Robert Alter translates the Hebrew here as "his face fell," in Robert Alter, *The Five Books of Moses.*

4. R. Kent Hughes, *Genesis, Beginning and Blessing* (Preaching the Word) (Wheaton, IL: Crossway, 2004), 104.

5. I first read this idea in Charles R. Swindoll, ed., *The Living Insights Study Bible*, First Printing edition (Grand Rapids, MI: Zondervan, 1996), 9. It has gripped me ever since.

6. Quoted in *CSB Spurgeon Study Bible* (Nashville, TN: Holman Bible Publishers, 2017), 8.

7. Atkinson, *The Message of Genesis 1–11* (Downers Grove, IL: InterVarsity Press: 1990), 114.

Chapter 6 ✦ The Conquering Seed: Seth, Enoch, Lamech, and the Promise of God

1. Charles Wesley, 1739, altered by Martin Madan, 1760, in *The Service of Song for Baptist Churches* (New York: Sheldon and Company, 1876), 97.

2. This sermon by Matt Chandler at Village Church, an intro to the book of Revelation, helped awaken me to this idea of Christmas in Heaven. Eric Boggs, "Introduction"—TVC Resources, accessed July 31, 2021, https://www.tvcresources.net/resource-library/sermons/introduction-3/.

3. Kenneth Matthews, *The New American Commentary: Genesis 1–11:26* (Nashville, TN: Holman Reference, 2016), 310.

4. John H. Walton, *The NIV Application Commentary: Genesis* (Grand Rapids, MI: Zondervan, 2001), 277.

5. Derek Kidner, *Genesis: An Introduction and Commentary* (London: Tyndale, 1967), 83.

6. Ibid., 82.

7. "Seth Definition and Meaning—Bible Dictionary," biblestudytools.com, accessed August 4, 2021, https://www.biblestudytools.com/dictionary/seth/.

8. Andrew Louth, ed., *Genesis 1–11: Ancient Christian Commentary on Scripture (Old Testament, vol. 1)* (Downers Grove, IL: InterVarsity Press, 2001), 114.

9. Mitchell L. Chase, "The Genesis of Resurrection Hope: Exploring Its Early Presence and Deep Roots," *Journal of the Evangelical Theological Society* 57–3: 473, accessed August 3, 2021, https://www.etsjets.org/files/JETS-PDFs/57/57-3/JETS_57-3_467-80_Chase.pdf.

10. Tony Evans, *One Family Under God* (Chicago: Moody, 2013), 30.

11. R. Kent Hughes, *Genesis, Beginning and Blessing* (Preaching the Word) (Wheaton, IL: Crossway, 2012), 120.

12. *CSB Spurgeon Study Bible* (Nashville, TN: Holman Bible Publishers, 2017), 10.

13. Sandra L. Richter, *The Epic of Eden: A Christian Entry into the Old Testament* (Downers Grove, IL: InterVarsity Press, 2010), 135.

Chapter 7 ✦ The Depraved: The Mysterious Madness of the Nephilim

1. R. Kent Hughes, *Genesis: Beginning and Blessing* (Preaching the Word) (Wheaton, IL: Crossway, 2012), 126.

2. G. K. Beale and D. A. Carson, *Commentary on the New Testament Use of the Old Testament* (Grand Rapids, MI: Baker Academic, 2007), 1048.
   Several modern scholars also hold to this view, as well as many more recent scholars and teachers such as D. A. Carson, Kent Hughes, Gordon Wenham, John McArthur, Tom Schreiner, Peter Gentry, Rick Phillips, and others.

3. Thomas R. Schreiner, *1 & 2 Peter and Jude* (New American Commentary) (Nashville, TN: Holman Reference, 2003), 453–54.

4. Derek Kidner, *Genesis: An Introduction and Commentary* (London: Tyndale, 1967), 89. See also, Southern Seminary, *Were the Sons of God in Genesis 6 Fallen Angels? Who Were the Nephilim?*, accessed August 6, 2021, https://www.youtube.com/watch?app=desktop&v=qKtHwc3mMY8&feature=youtu.be.

5. *Genesis*, Calvin's Commentaries, vol. 1, trans. and rev. by John King (Grand Rapids, MI: Baker Academic, 1999), 238.

6. *Luther's Works*, vol. 1, Jaroslav Jan Pelikan, gen. ed. (St. Louis: Concordia Publishing House, 1958), 10–15. Several more modern scholars hold to this view, including Wayne Grudem, Warren Wiersbe, Kevin DeYoung, John Murray, R. C. Sproul, and Kenneth Matthews.

7. Gordon J. Wenham, *Genesis 1–15, Volume 1* (Word Biblical Commentary) (Grand Rapids, MI: Zondervan Academic, 2014), 141.

8. "Giants in the Land: A Biblical Theology of the Nephilim, Anakim, Rephaim (and Goliath)," Knowing Scripture, accessed August 7, 2021, https://knowingscripture .com/articles/giants-in-the-land-a-biblical-theology-of-the-nephilim-anakim-rephaim-and-goliath.

9. Wenham, *Genesis 1–15*, 143.

Chapter 8 ✦ The Preacher: Noah's Lonely Courage, and a Flood That Saves

1. James Montgomery Boice, *Genesis: An Expositional Commentary, Vol. 1: Genesis 1–11* (Grand Rapids, MI: Baker Books, 1998), 319.

2. Andrew Louth, ed., *Genesis 1–11: Ancient Christian Commentary on Scripture (Old Testament, vol. 1)* (Downers Grove, IL: InterVarsity Press, 2001), 123.

3. Gordon J. Wenham, *Genesis 1–15, Volume 1* (Word Biblical Commentary) (Grand Rapids, MI: Zondervan Academic, 2014), 144.

4. Ibid., 144.

5. Ibid., 172.

6. Charles R. Swindoll, ed., *The Living Insights Study Bible*, First Printing edition (Grand Rapids, MI: Zondervan, 1996), 1340.

7. Henry M. Morris, *The Genesis Record: A Scientific and Devotional Commentary on the Book of Beginnings* (Grand Rapids, MI: Baker Book House, 1976), 183.

8. Joe Carter, "9 Things You Should Know about the Story of Noah," The Gospel Coalition, May 2, 2014, https://www.thegospelcoalition.org/article/9-things-you-should-know-about-the-story-of-noah/.

9. D. Martyn Lloyd-Jones, *Expository Sermons on 2 Peter* (Edinburgh: Banner of Truth, 1999), 151–54.

10. R. Albert Mohler Jr., *Exalting Jesus in Hebrews* (Christ-Centered Exposition Commentary) (Nashville, TN: Holman Reference, 2017), 176.

11. Wenham, *Genesis 1–15*, 172.

12. *NIV Zondervan Study Bible* (Grand Rapids, MI: Zondervan), 2018.

13. Mohler, *Exalting Jesus in Hebrews*, 177.

14. Bruce K. Waltke, *Genesis: A Commentary* (Grand Rapids, MI: Zondervan Academic, 2016), 157.

15. Sandra L. Richter, *The Epic of Eden: A Christian Entry into the Old Testament* (Downers Grove, IL: InterVarsity Press, 2010), 146.

Chapter 9 ✦ The Descendants: Shem, Ham,
Japheth, and God's New Creation

1. "God Remembered Noah," April 14, 2006, https://www.ligonier.org/learn/devotionals/god-remembered-noah.
2. Sandra L. Richter, *The Epic of Eden: A Christian Entry into the Old Testament* (Downers Grove, IL: InterVarsity Press, 2010), 144.
3. David J. Atkinson, *The Message of Genesis 1–11* (InterVarsity Press, 2017), 164.
4. Warren W. Wiersbe, *Be Basic* (Genesis 1–11) (Colorado Springs, CO: David C. Cook), 135.
5. Quoted in *CSB Spurgeon Study Bible* (Nashville, TN: Holman Bible Publishers, 2017), 14.
6. R. Kent Hughes, *Genesis, Beginning and Blessing* (Preaching the Word) (Wheaton, IL: Crossway, 2004), 150.
7. Kenneth Matthews, *The New American Commentary: Genesis 1–11:26* (Nashville, TN: Holman Reference, 2016), 172.
8. *CSB Tony Evans Study Bible* (Nashville, TN: Holman Bible Publishers, 2019).
9. Bruce K. Waltke, *Genesis: A Commentary* (Grand Rapids, MI: Zondervan, 2001), 153.

Daniel Darling is a bestselling author of eleven books, including *The Characters of Christmas*, *The Characters of Easter*, *The Dignity Revolution*, and *A Way with Words*. He has pastored churches in Illinois and Tennessee and served as an executive with multiple denominational and parachurch organizations. He currently serves as director of the Land Center for Cultural Engagement at Southwestern Baptist Theological Seminary. He and his wife Angela have four children and reside in the Dallas/Fort Worth area.

Learn Something New this Christmas

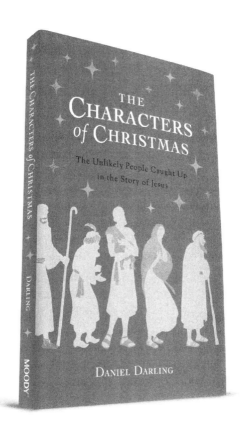

This year, enter into the stories of the minor and not-so-minor characters who played a part in Jesus' birth, and see the most important character—Jesus Christ—with new eyes. And with discussion questions and a Christmas song suggestion for each chapter, it's perfect for engaging your whole family.

978-0-8024-1929-3 | also available as eBook and audiobook

A New Look at the Ancient Story of Easter

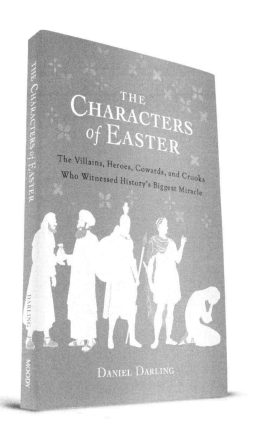

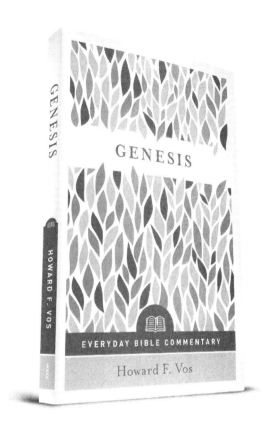